OSCAR WILDE AND MYSELF

Yours Very truly
Alfred Douglas

OSCAR WILDE
AND MYSELF

BY

LORD ALFRED DOUGLAS

WITH PORTRAIT OF THE AUTHOR
AND THIRTEEN OTHER PORTRAITS AND ILLUSTRATIONS
ALSO FAC-SIMILE LETTERS

New York
Duffield & Company
1914

Preface

THE manuscript of this book was completed by me and handed over to the publishers as long ago as last July. Certain persons thereupon deemed it advisable to apply to the Court for an injunction restraining me from including in my book any of the letters from Oscar Wilde which were in my possession, and they further applied for an injunction restraining me from quoting from the unpublished portion of the "De Profundis" manuscript which is now sealed up at the British Museum and which was used against me in open Court as part of the justification in the defence to a libel action brought by me in April, 1913. The application for these injunctions was made in the Vacation Court before Mr. Justice Astbury, the most recent recruit to the Judicial Bench. It was immediately granted, and though I was advised by counsel to appeal against the

decision, I thought it better to accept it, at any rate
for the moment. Consequently, all the copious
extracts I was intending to publish from the " De
Profundis," which extracts had already been reproduced in all the newspapers at the hearing of the
action of Douglas *v.* Ransome and The Times
Book Club have been entirely removed. The same
applies to those letters of Wilde's which I had
originally included in my book. As far as the letters are concerned, the omission does not very
much affect the book. The letters were included
not to make points against my opponents, but
merely as interesting curiosities. The enforced
omission of the extracts from the unpublished "De
Profundis" has, on the other hand, been an undoubted handicap to me. A considerable portion
of this book is devoted to a reply to the violently
mendacious attacks made upon me and upon my
family by Wilde in that unpublished portion of the
" De Profundis" which has been accepted by the
authorities of the British Museum from the literary
executor of the late author. Obviously it is very
difficult to reply to an attack which one is unable
to quote, and I can only say that I have met the

difficulty as best I could, and that at a future date I look forward to being able to deal with the whole matter even more completely and finally. In this connection I refer my readers to the chapter in this book entitled " A Challenge to Mr. Ross."

ALFRED BRUCE DOUGLAS

Boulogne-sur-Mer

April, 1914

To my Mother
Sibyl, Marchioness of Queensberry

Contents

Contents

List of Illustrations

OSCAR WILDE AND MYSELF

Introductory

OUT of little things there may come a peck of troubles. I suppose that my first meeting with Oscar Wilde was to me, at that time, a little thing. By this I do not mean that I was other than glad to meet a man of Wilde's culture and attainments, but I was not particularly impressed by him at first, and, if I had never set eyes on him, I should certainly have lost nothing. As Fate arranges matters, our acquaintance has brought the gravest disasters, not only upon myself, but upon those nearest and dearest to me. The purpose of the present book is not to complain of what had happened or to rail against Oscar Wilde, who, for years, was my close friend and who, at one time in our friendship, held me fascinated by what I conceived to be his genius. That he had what passed for genius nobody will, I think, nowadays dispute, though it used to be the fashion to pooh-pooh him for a mere *poseur* and decadent. If our friendship had remained a private friendship—

like many other of Wilde's friendships—instead of being bruited abroad from every housetop, this book would never have been written. From the moment Wilde's name became notorious, however, people have been careful to link our names together, and even more careful to link them together in scandalous ways. There are many persons now alive who were friends with Wilde in the days of his greatness and prosperity; and, without a single exception, so far as I am aware, their friendship is reckoned to their credit, and, in some instances, has proved highly advantageous to them from many points of view. Yet what was a virtue in these persons would seem to have been a crime in me. I have never boasted of my relations with Wilde and, though I have had many proposals from editors and publishers to say my say about my friend for handsome remuneration, I have never previously taken a penny piece from any of them. I have always known that there was nothing in our friendship of which I need be ashamed and, although the tongue of malice and slander has been busy with my name almost without ceasing since the day of Wilde's downfall, I looked to time and the facts to set me right.

Since Wilde's downfall, my life has been lived under conditions of which it is to be hoped few persons have had experience. Always I have had to fight the cunningly contrived innuendo which, while it could not be nailed to the counter and rebutted in the Courts of Law, nevertheless did its deadly work and threw its bitter odium over my name and fame. On occasions out of number I have had to take expensive legal proceedings in sheer self-defence. Generally, the parties concerned have been people of straw, who apologised abjectly or disappeared or got out by asserting that they did not mean what they had tried to say, immediately the writs were issued. My own determination has always been to refrain from litigation on the subject, unless it were absolutely forced upon me. How far I was wise in this determination is another affair.

It may seem a simple and easy thing to wipe out slander. How difficult it is, only the few persons who have had a really foul and abominable slander put up against them can know. In addition to the multitudinous gentlemen with ready pens who have not scrupled to decry and defame me, I have for years had to contend with the class of persons who had letters to sell or letters to print, and who have ever been handy with their documents and "inside information" when opportunity might arise whereby they hoped to turn an honest penny. For these gentry I have encouraged a proper contempt, and not one of them has had from me a single sixpence or a breath of appeal for the mercy which they believed themselves capable of extending. Later, a Mr. Arthur Ransome—whom I had not known as an acquaintance of Wilde and who had no acquaintance with myself—went out of his way to assert in a book, which purported to be an intimate study of Wilde, that the latter had attributed some measure of his public obloquy to my influence over him; and, further, that I had lived upon Wilde after his imprisonment and left him stranded at Naples when his financial resources were exhausted. I took an action for libel against Ransome and his publishers and The Times Book Club, with the result that the publishers withdrew Ransome's book from circulation, leaving him and The Times Book Club to make what defence they could. The jury found for the defendants on the first libel, and that the second libel was not a libel at all. It will interest all parties concerned to know that this is exactly the finding which I anticipated, and it is noteworthy that the libels of which I complained have been expunged from the new edition of the book. Mr. Justice Darling and the defendants' counsel repeatedly observed during the course of the trial that they could not understand what motive had prompted me to come into court. A letter which Wilde addressed to me previous to his imprisonment, and other letters which I had written to him, were read by defendants' counsel. Judge, counsel and jury alike appear to have imagined that, if I had known of the existence of these letters, I should not have brought my action. In point of fact, I was well aware of their existence and I was told, while the action was still pending, that they were to be raked up and that I should be "simply eviscerated" in the witness-box. Well, I went like a lamb to the evisceration, and Mr. Justice Darling marvelled at my lack of worldly wisdom.

In the following pages I shall set out the whole details of my relationship with Oscar Wilde, and I do so, not by way of defence or apology—because I need neither—but simply with a view to making clear in the public interest, and for the benefit of posterity, the true inwardness of Wilde's writing and character. I take this step as much for Wilde's sake as for my own.

During his imprisonment at Reading, Oscar Wilde was permitted the use of pen and ink, and he appears to have relieved the tedium of his incarceration by writing eighty thousand words, or thereabouts, addressed to myself. A copy of the manuscript is alleged to have been sent to me by post, shortly after its completion. Half of it has been published under the ægis of Mr. Robert Ross, and is known to the world as "De Profundis." The nature and drift of the published portion of the MSS. needs no comment from me at this juncture. The unpublished parts, however, may reasonably be described as a frantic attack upon me. Till a copy of this attack came into my hands during the time the Ransome action was pending, I had no knowledge of its existence. At the trial, it transpired that this farrago of hysterical abuse had been handed by Mr. Ross to the authorities at the British Museum as a present to the nation, and that it was not to be made public till 1960, when it is to be hoped we shall all be dead. I could have wished, for the sake of my old friend, that Mr. Ross had seen the wisdom of destroying a piece of writing which even Mr. Justice Darling conceives to be evil and discreditable to its author. Whether or not it is my property is a legal problem. I have applied to the British Museum for its return, but so far without success. Mr. Ross's "present to the nation" may possibly abide on the British Museum's shelves, unperused by the curious, till 1960. My own present to Mr. Ross and to the weeping worshippers of Wilde is delivered herewith, and can be opened and read by him who runs while we have still a little breath. The result of Mr. Ross's action would seem to be that, if the British Museum do, in fact, disclose the contents of the manuscript after my death Wilde will be disgraced and confounded on his own evidence.

Oscar Wilde and Myself

CHAPTER I

OXFORD

A FTER leaving Winchester, where I won the school steeplechase and edited a paper called the *Pentagram*—the only literary or journalistic venture, by the way, out of which I ever made a profit—I went up to Oxford in the ordinary course. I was entered at Magdalen College, and I remained an undergraduate of the University for four years. Magdalen, as it always has been in recent times, and still continues to be, was considered a more or less fashionable college. It was the never-ending boast of Oscar Wilde that he had been there. The continuous "when I was at Oxford" which crops up in his writings was complemented by continuous "when I was at Magdalen" in his conversation. I do not know that there was anything extraordinary about Magdalen in my time. I look back upon my life there as fairly pleasant, and chiefly so because I had the companionship of my friend, the late Viscount Encombe, whose death at the early age of twenty-eight was a great blow to me. Of course, I met at Oxford all the people who were supposed to be worth meeting. There was Mr. Warren, then, as now, President of Magdalen, whom I remember on account of his black beard and his very obsequious treatment of myself. He was a profound admirer of Matthew Arnold, whose poetry he urged me to study and imitate. He also, rather incongruously, professed great admiration for the writings of his personal friend, John Addington Symonds. I say "incongruously;" for an admiration for Matthew Arnold ought surely to preclude an admiration for Symonds, at any rate, as far as poetry is concerned.

For Oscar Wilde he also admitted a great partiality. They had been contemporaries at the University in their undergraduate days and, to a certain extent, friends. When Wilde came up to see me at Oxford, he always made a point of calling on Mr. Warren, and on these occasions I invariably accompanied him, and I thus had the advantage of profiting by their conversation, which, needless to say, generally turned on literary matters; but I cannot honestly say that I was greatly edified or that any gems of purest ray serene from these duologues have remained shining in my memory. When I first became an intimate friend of Oscar Wilde, my mother, who had an instinctive dislike of Wilde, wrote to Mr. Warren and asked him if he considered Wilde was the sort of man who would be a good friend for me. The President, in reply, sent her a long letter in which he gave Wilde a very high character, praised his great gifts and achievements of scholarship and literature, and assured her that I might consider myself lucky to have obtained the favourable notice of such an eminent man. I mention this, not as anything to Mr. Warren's detriment, but simply to show the sort of reputation Wilde at that time enjoyed among the big-wigs of the University.

Then there was Walter Pater, to whom I was introduced by Wilde on the first occasion when the latter visited me at Oxford. Wilde had an immense opinion of Pater and spoke of him always with reverence as the greatest living writer of prose. I tried hard to appreciate Pater and he personally was kind to me, but quite apart from the fact that he had practically no conversation and would sit for hours without saying more than an occasional word, I never could bring myself to have more than a very limited admiration for his far-famed prose, which has always seemed to me artificial, finnicking and over-elaborated to an exasperating degree. I have altogether livelier recollections of

Mr., now the Reverend Dr. Bussell, Pater's most intimate friend at Brazenose, for he was a fine musician and had a devotion to Handel and Bach which endears his memory to me to this day.

Next to Encombe, probably my best friend among the undergraduates of my day was the poet Lionel Johnson, a frail, tiny man, with probably the finest head and the kindest heart in the University. We talked and wrote a considerable amount of poetry together, and it was Johnson who introduced me to Oscar Wilde. At this period Wilde had just begun to be considered a person of some promise in letters. He had outgrown "æsthetics" and had written "The Picture of Dorian Gray" and "Intentions," and was rehearsing his first play: *Lady Windermere's Fan.*

One vacation I went with Johnson to Wilde's house in Tite Street, and over dinner commenced a friendship which was to be none too fortunate for either of us. For some reason or other Wilde insisted on being considerably more brilliant that evening than ever he was afterwards. Indeed, he fired off witticisms so persistently and with such an evident anxiety not to miss even the slenderest of opportunities that, while I had come to the meeting in the spirit of the youthful admirer, or literary hero-worshipper, I went away with a sort of feeling that I had been at a show and that I had not seen a really great man after all. However, as our acquaintance ripened, I began to understand, or imagine that I understood, Wilde's moods. I soon perceived that he said quite half of everything he had to say with his tongue in his cheek and that one should not really take him seriously, because his only aim in conversation was not to say what he believed, but to say what he supposed to be witty, profound, whimsical or brilliant at the moment. Further, I soon discovered that Wilde was one of those conversationalists who were conscious of the value, not only of their own *mots,* but of those of other people, and that his or my joke or epigram let loose over lunch on Monday was bound to figure in the bit of dialogue or portion of an essay which he would indite, with the help of stiff whiskies-and-sodas and illimitable cigarettes, on a Tuesday morning. At the same time, I cheerfully admit that I found him an agreeable, entertaining and even lovable acquaintance. He had, of course, an eye for humour and beauty, he was a great deal of a scholar, he spoke good English and excellent French, and he had a pleasant voice and a charming delivery. Compared with the average man-about-town he shone, and compared with the average "man of genius" he scintillated.

During my second year at Oxford I contributed to the *Oxford Magazine,* the official journal of the University, a poem which pleased everybody but its author and provoked the excellent Mr. Warren to write me a lengthy letter of praise and congratulation. Unfortunately, I have not got this epistle at hand, otherwise I might be tempted to print it with a view of convincing the University Oxford that I am indeed somewhat of a poet. This was the first serious poem I ever wrote or, at any rate, preserved, and it is now included in the "City of the Soul." I also contributed on several occasions to an undergraduate paper called *The Spirit Lamp,* which was owned by a man whose name I forget, but he called on me one day and explained that he was going down and very munificently offered to make me a present of his journalistic property if, as he diffidently put it, I cared to take it on and would promise to continue its high traditions to the best of my ability. I gave this gentleman the necessary assurances, and *The Spirit Lamp* became mine. Six or seven subsequent numbers appeared under my editorship, and copies of these numbers are, I understand, worth considerably more than their published price in what is known as the market. Of my own contributions I have a poor opinion, though they were warmly appreciated at the time of their appearance by that class of person who makes warm appreciations a sort of hobby. I am proud of the fact, however, that I printed some of Lionel Johnson's best verses and several contributions from the late John Addington Symonds, and I also had the advantage of various contributions from Wilde, including his prose poems "The Disciple" and "The House of Judgment," and what I consider to be the best sonnet he ever wrote. Wilde frequently came to Oxford in those days, and on several occasions stayed as my guest in the rooms in High Street which I shared with my friend, Lord Encombe.

Although throughout my career as an undergraduate I was keenly interested in poetry and letters generally, I did not profess to belong to any literary set and I had no notion of taking to writing as a profession. My name and family traditions marked me out for the sporting and convivial side of University life rather than for serious literary endeavour. I read for the Honours school in a desultory kind of way, but relieved the tedium of my prescribed studies by a good deal of riding and boating and fairly regular attendance at such race-meetings as were within reasonable distance of what Mr. Ruskin doubtless called his Alma Mater. At the same time, my interest in poetry was well

known in the University, and I was considered a
poet of promise and parts.

Of course, every undergraduate who can write
poetry at all is expected to compete for the Newdigate prize. I was frequently urged by my friends
to enter for this prize, but none of the subjects set
during my first three years at Oxford appealed to
me. Tennyson, if I remember rightly, won the
Newdigate with a poem about Timbuctoo. Such
a subject while, perhaps, entertaining enough in
its way, is, obviously, not very inspiring and certainly not calculated to induce the production of
high poetry. As I have said, the subjects set in
my first three years did not excite in me any great
poetical emotion. In my fourth year, however, the
subject was St. Francis of Assisi, and I felt at once
that here was my opportunity. I told my friends
that I should enter, and began to plan the poem. I
was talking of the matter at dinner one night, with
Encombe and the late Lord Warkworth—afterwards Earl Percy, who was at that time at Christ-
church—and I told the latter that I was going in
for the prize. He said that he, too, was having
a shot at it, and pointed out that it was impossible
for me to enter as I was in my fourth year. He
offered to show me the rule in the Statutes, but,
unfortunately, we had not a copy handy and I took

it that Warkworth knew what he was talking about and let the thing drop. Lord Warkworth won the Newdigate that year himself, and it was only after the announcement of his success that I discovered that there was no such rule as the one he had told me of. Of course, I make no aspersion on Warkworth's good intentions in the matter; yet, in a sense, it is a pity that I did not look more closely into the rules, because, though I say it myself, I could have beaten him with a good many lengths to spare, and though to have won the Newdigate means, perhaps, very little from a literary point of view, it appears to be a good backing for a man who goes in seriously for poetry.

I have noticed with some astonishment that whenever opportunity has arisen persons who do not love me have been at pains to suggest that there was something discreditable about my Oxford career. It has been hinted that I was "sent down" in disgrace, and great capital has been made of the circumstance that I left Oxford without a degree. In point of fact, I was "sent down" in my second year for a term because I was "ploughed" in my examination for "smalls," and I soon set this right by spending three weeks with a crammer and getting myself well posted up in Euclid and such-like subjects, which, though doubtless very important in their way, had never specially attracted me. When the time came for my examination in the Honours school I happened to be ill and was unable to attend, so that I left the University degreeless. Without any suggestion from me, the authorities offered to confer an honorary degree upon me if I cared to return in the vacation and pass two papers. I consulted my father, the late Marquis of Queensberry, on the subject, and he told me that he had never known a degree to be worth twopence to anybody, and, accordingly, I never took the trouble to avail myself of the Oxford's kind offer. If going down without a degree is a crime, I belong to an excellent company of criminals, for Swinburne left Oxford minus a degree and so did Lord Rosebery and, if it comes to genius, so did the poet Shelley.

I need hardly say that Oscar Wilde expressed himself as entirely delighted with my remissness in failing to become an M.A. Oxon. He said, in his usual airy way, that it was "wonderful" of me and a "distinction," and he pointed out that I should be like Swinburne, who determined to remain an undergraduate all his life. I am free to confess that personally I did not take much interest in the matter either way, though, had I understood the world then as I understand it now, I might have been a trifle less careless.

OSCAR WILDE

Generally, I do not wish it to be supposed that my life at Oxford was any more immaculate than that of other young men in my own position in life. I came into collision with the authorities on various small sins of omission and commission. I was gated once for going to the Derby—wicked youth that I was!—and I dare say I worried the authorities by my persistent refusal to take either themselves or the University for the most serious thing in nature. But I lived with them gloriously and delicately for the full undergraduate span of four years, save one term over "smalls," and, as I have shown, they were quite willing to take me to their bosom as a full member of the University if I had cared to fall into their embrace.

The idea that Oxford is a place entirely given over to the laborious and the assiduous pursuit of knowledge is a mistake. It can be proved quite easily that, while the assiduous and the laborious who choose to make Oxford a sort of career may do very well out of it in the way of Fellowships, scholastic appointments, and so forth, the best men Oxford turns out are, in the main, men who have been considered to have missed their opportunities. Everybody who was anybody at Oxford in my time had a disposition to be very modest about learning and a trifle shy about recommending it as the be-all

and end-all of life. There is a tale attributed to a
certain worthy Don—indeed, it is said to have been
his stock story—which relates to two excellent youths
of good family who went up to Oxford together.
One of them was slack and fond of his ease; he
read nothing and did nothing and, after years of
dissipation, was fain to get a living by driving a
hansom-cab. The other youth, the pride of his
family and college, read everything and won everything and did everything that was proper. Years
after, somebody found him in London doing his
best to keep the wolf from the door by driving a
four-wheeler. This is an old story, but it is a very
good one, and anybody who knows Oxford in the
intimate personal sense knows how true it may well
be. For myself, I think if it had come to cab-driving
the hansom would unquestionably have been my
vehicle.

I was careless and desultory in the widest sense
of the terms; so careless and desultory, in fact, that,
with a view to saving time and trouble in my intercourse with the authorities, I had a form printed as
follows:—

> Lord Alfred Bruce Douglas presents his
> compliments to.......................
> and regrets that he will be unable to
> ....in consequence of
> . . . .

Filled up, this ingenious document would read as follows:—

> Lord Alfred Bruce Douglas presents his compliments to Professor Smith and regrets that he will be unable to show up an essay on the Evolution of the Moral Idea in consequence of not having prepared one.

I found these missives extremely useful and used a great quantity. They were famed throughout the University and, though they angered some of the Dons to the verge of madness, nothing could be done about them, because they were obviously polite, and an undergraduate who is polite to his pastors and masters has done his duty. It may be on the strength of this form and on my being "sent down" for a failure to pass "smalls" that the legend and fiction of my alleged ignominious career at Oxford depends. I know of nothing more serious, otherwise I should be pleased to unburden myself. Both before and after I terminated my undergraduateship by removing my name from the books of Magdalen College, I was a frequent visitor to the scene of my old triumphs and kept up many friendships among the men of my time and among the University authorities. I removed my name from the books of my own free will and as a matter of personal convenience. What I did may have been a trifle unusual, though I am acquainted with at least one distinguished Oxford man who did precisely the same thing, and that my actions should have been twisted into a sort of horrible wickedness must have startled a good many other people besides myself.

So much for the gay Lord Alfred Douglas, under-graduate of Magdalen College, Oxford.

CHAPTER II

IT is very hard, indeed, wellnigh impossible, for me to recapture and set forth for the benefit of my readers the secret of the fascination that Oscar Wilde had for me in those far-off days. The revelation of his perfidy and vileness which came to me when, about a year ago, I first got knowledge of the existence of the unpublished portion of "De Profundis," the shock of horror, indignation and disgust which the reading of that abominable document produced in my mind, and the ever-recurring reflection that during the last few years of his life and after his release from prison, when he was professing the greatest friendship and affection for me and living—for a time in part, and ultimately altogether—on my bounty, he was all the while the secret author of a foul and lying attack on me and on my family which he had arranged to make public after my death, combine to make the task of reconstructing a semblance of my old feeling for him almost a hopeless one. Long however before

I had cognisance of the unpublished "De Profundis," my view of his character and my estimate of his value as a man of letters had undergone a profound change. With the passing of the years and a more serious and mature outlook on the facts of life and on the responsibilities of those who seek the suffrages or merely the ears of the general reader, I had arrived at the conclusion that Oscar Wilde's writings were ridiculously overrated, that he was never either a great poet or a great writer of prose, and that the harm he had caused to the whole body of English literature and the pernicious effect he had exercised on the literary movements and the journalism of the period immediately succeeding his own, very much more than counterbalanced the credit of any legitimate success he may have achieved. Still, up till the period when the discovery of the unpublished part of "De Profundis" was forced upon my notice, I carefully refrained from giving voice to these sentiments. The man had been my friend, I had been very fond of him, and I had formerly had an exaggerated view as to the value of his work. I did not therefore consider that I was in any way called upon to interfere with his literary reputation, even though, in my opinion, it was a specious reputation and the result, moreover, of a cleverly-engineered campaign

on his behalf, made by friends who were more careful of Wilde's fame than of the general good of
letters.

Still less did I conceive it to be any part of my
duty to attack what was left of his character. On
the contrary, I steadily persisted in taking the best
view possible of the man, and until I read the unpublished "De Profundis" I kept a great measure
of my affection for his memory and, in common
with many other people, cherished fond illusions
about his moral character. That my affection for
him was real and sincere and continued to be so
right up to the time when I read the unpublished
part of "De Profundis" is fairly proved by the facts
that I persistently defended him—even at the cost
of some violence to my own literary conscience—in
the columns of the *Academy,* when I was its editor,
and that I wrote to his memory one of my best
sonnets, which I here reproduce:—

The Dead Poet

I dreamed of him last night, I saw his face
All radiant and unshadowed of distress,
And as of old, in music measureless,
I heard his golden voice and marked him trace
Under the common thing the hidden grace,
And conjure wonder out of emptiness,
Till mean things put on beauty like a dress
And all the world was an enchanted place.

And then methought outside a fast locked gate
I mourned the loss of unrecorded words,
Forgotten tales and mysteries half said,
Wonders that might have been articulate,
And voiceless thoughts like murdered singing birds.
And so I woke and knew that he was dead.

Now I wrote that sonnet as long ago as 1901, within a few months of Wilde's death, but I included it in my 1909 volume of sonnets and, in face of it, I could not possibly pretend, even if I wished to do so, that I was not at one time deeply attached to him and that I continued to cherish his memory after his death. But when it comes to explaining that attachment and reproducing the atmosphere which generated it, I find that I am met at the outset by this deplorable set-back—namely and to wit: that the very qualities in him which then excited my admiration, now evoke my contempt. It must be remembered that when I met Wilde I was very young in years, and still younger in temperament and in experience. I was, in fact, a mere child. I reproduce on the opposite page a photograph of myself, taken in my second year at Oxford, just about the time I first met Wilde. It is obviously the photograph of a boy—and a fairly unsophisticated boy, at that. There are numbers of my friends and contemporaries at Oxford, now living, and they could all bear witness to the fact that even at the age of

twenty-three I had the appearance of a youth of
sixteen; and though, of course, I should have been
woefully offended if any one had told me so at the
time, there was much in my character that corre-
sponded with my appearance. I don't think there
was ever any one so easily deceived, such an obvious
mark for the designing, as I was in those days. I
was never allowed to forget that I was Lord Alfred
Douglas, the son of a marquis and a person of consequence. The mere fact that I thought myself
very knowing and a complete man of the world only
served to make me an easier victim to any accomplished teller of the literary tale. Wilde made a
dead set at me. He was attracted by my youth, my
guilelessness, and—to be perfectly frank—by what
he considered my social importance, and he laid
himself out to captivate me and to fascinate me.

He was then about forty years of age; he was a
brilliant talker—every one admits that: I have
never heard it denied, even by his greatest enemy;
he was utterly unlike any one or anything that
I had ever come across before, and he had that sort
of assumption of certainty about all the problems
of life which is one of the compensations—ex-
changed for many other better things—that comes
at that age to an accomplished man of the world.
He had a habit of enunciating the most entirely

unmoral and subversive sentiments in a manner
and with an air of final authority which could not
fail to appeal to a high-spirited youth, already in-
clined—as is the manner of high-spirited youth—
to kick over the traces. According to him, it didn't
matter in the least what one did as long as one
happened to be "a charming and graceful young
man, related to every one in the peerage," and did
whatever one wanted to do in "a charming and
graceful manner." This "simple and beautiful"
theory appealed irresistibly to me, as it very well
might to any thoughtless youth; and, coming as
it did from one who was actually looked up to and
admired by the President of my College, and who
had been commended to my mother as a most desirable acquaintance for me, it naturally seemed the
last word of wisdom. But how can I be expected
now to have anything but contempt for such arts,
practised by a clever man of the world on an unre-
flecting boy? Or how can I be blamed because the
recollection of the fact that I was, for the time,
attracted by such preposterous and poisonous spe-
ciousness is anything else but repugnant to me now
when I look back on it?

In my desperate anxiety to do justice to the memory of one who was formerly my friend, I might

LORD ALFRED DOUGLAS, AT THE AGE OF TWENTY-ONE,
AT OXFORD

be tempted to give more instances of his method of
dealing with young men whose good will he was
anxious to obtain; but by so doing I should add
nothing to his reputation, even for cleverness. It
is the easiest thing in the world to turn the head
of a young fellow at Oxford or Cambridge. Any
man of the world could do so, if he cared to take
the trouble and was sufficiently unscrupulous. It
does not require great wit or great brains or anything but impudence and a blunted sense of honour.
These two "qualities" Wilde undoubtedly possessed.

It is easy for any one who has not forgotten the
time of his own youth to see how Wilde contrived
to attract me. He flattered me incessantly, he professed extreme admiration for the few poetical
efforts which I had then produced—efforts, by the
way, which, in his Reading Gaol days, became poor
"undergraduate verses"—and whatever I did or
whatever I said was "wonderful" in his eyes. He
displayed all the outward signs and symbols of
friendship and affection. He has himself set them
all out faithfully, so that I am spared the necessity
of reproducing them here. I will merely put it on
record—to give him the whole of the credit that
can possibly be due to him—that, in the matter of
sending expensive bunches of muscat grapes and
copies of the illustrated papers to my bedside when

I happened to be ill, promptly replying to requests for an immediate despatch of cigarettes when I had gone away to the country and forgotten to take them with me, and remembering my favourite dishes when I happened to dine with him, he was "all that a loving heart could wish." I accepted these husks for the real bread of friendship, and because it has been all through my life my fatal habit to idealise my friends and to endow them with all sorts of qualities which they never dreamed of possessing, I conceived a great and lasting affection for this man; and, when he was in trouble, I fought for him and defended him through thick and thin and without any regard to rhyme or reason or my own interest. Hence these tears! And I am not in the least disposed to dispute that I have only myself to blame and that it served me very well right. "But this is got by casting pearl to hogs."

CHAPTER III

IN view of the curious anxiety of those who support and uphold the Wilde legend, to paint him for us as a man of fashion and social position, it may be interesting if I try to recall Oscar Wilde in his figure as a buck or, as we nowadays say, man about town. There can be no doubt whatever that he did really consider himself a person of fashion and social standing, outside of his claims to literary notoriety.

In his writings he is very fond of using such phrases as "men of our rank," "people of our social class," and so forth. "Rank" is a good word, and Wilde knew perfectly well how to use it in a manner which would lead people really to believe that he was nobly born. He was able to talk of his mother as Lady Wilde, and I have heard him refer to her in certain company as "her ladyship" with great effect. You would imagine from his manner that she was a *grande dame* of the first water, with two or three large places to her name, and retinues of servants.

Of Papa Wilde we did not hear quite so frequently, probably for the reason that he was not "his lordship." At the same time, Wilde could not have put on greater airs than he was sometimes wont to don if his father had been a duke.

Now, with this feeling of "family" about him, it is not extraordinary that he should have tried to live up to it to the best of his lights. He opined that if "a gentleman of rank" is to be taken for a gentleman of rank, he must not only keep his rank duly prominent in his conversation, but he must also look, dress and, as far as possible, live the part. In the matter of looks, Wilde believed in his heart that he had the "bulge" of all the literary people of his time. Tennyson might wear prophetic robes and wideawake hats, Swinburne might look the decent little ginger gentleman he was, Pater might pass for the profound and beetle-browed thinker on the high arts, Bernard Shaw might pass for the bewhiskered fire-eater, Arthur Symons for the blonde angel, Beardsley for the delicate spider-legged artist; but when it came to nobility and beauty of features, Wilde was convinced that he had them all "beaten to a frazzle." He was very fond of likening himself to the Roman Emperors. He had a big face, which was, as he himself put it, "delicately chiselled"; and if anybody

had asked him to sit for a bust of Nero, he would
have considered that person most discerning. I
remember him saying to me that, while it was considered among "the dull English" to be almost criminal for a man to speak of good looks, either in himself or in another man, good looks were half the
battle in society. Of course, I laughed and told him
not to be a fool; but he meant it, all the same; and
nothing would make him angrier than the hint that
his mouth was too large or that his face was spoiled
by too great an expanse of jowl. He took great
care of his complexion, and I never knew a man
who brushed his hair more frequently in the day
than he did.

He had a defect which was the sorrow of his life
—the arts of the dentist not being so well understood then as they are to-day—but on this I do not
propose to dwell.

I have been astonished that the published part
of "De Profundis" contains no touching and beautiful passages relating to clothes; and this is all the
more surprising because, in point of fact, Wilde
was, to a large extent, a tailor's man. I sometimes
think that if he had lived in the present era of
Homburg hats and tweed suits he would never have
been famous at all. He began his notoriety by fan-
tastic dressing, but as he ascended on the rungs

of art to the heaven of rank, his great aim was for what he termed "elegant correctness." Hence, the Wilde of my time consisted, to a great extent, of silk hat, frock coat, striped trousers and patent leather boots. Add to these a very tall clouded cane with a heavy gold knob and a pair of grey suede gloves, and you have the outward man. On the whole, I believe that he loathed the get-up, especially in the hot weather, but he stuck to it like a Trojan, and nobody ever saw Oscar Wilde in London outside of the regulation harness from eleven o'clock till seven, or outside of the hard white shirt and swallow-tails from seven-thirty till any time you like in the morning.

Being a Roman, he must do as persons of rank did in Rome, and he always struck me as being garbed in perpetual readiness to walk out or dine out with the duke or prince of the blood who would one day surely be calling round for him. He had a large turquoise set in diamonds, which I had purchased for him in an expansive moment when we happened to be together in a jeweller's shop. The occasion was his birthday and I took him to choose his own present. His eye fell on this sea-blue bauble in its ring of brilliants, and all question of trouble to the shopman was sunk. He wore this ornament in his shirt-front of evenings with a truly regal dignity. For myself, I used to call it "the blue light" or the "Hope-Not"—the Hope diamond being at that time very much to the fore in polite conversation.

In the country he naturally subsided into easier habiliments; but even here he must follow the fashion or be a little bit ahead of it. His suits and caps must be all of one piece, his boots as worn by "the nobility and gentry" and his general accoutrements designed subtly to convey the impression that he owned at least ten thousand acres somewhere or other.

This bucolic perfection was entirely a social affair with him, for he was most coy of being photographed otherwise than *en grande tenue.* In all his official photographs, the frock coat, braided for preference, or the fur coat, with a suggestion of a silk hat on a side table, "bear the gree."

The very suggestion of "literalism" in the matter of appearance horrified him. He desired to pass for a gentleman, a "gentleman of rank," and nothing more. And this he undoubtedly succeeded in doing to his own satisfaction. In his intercourse with the "highest in the land"—which was, to put it plainly, of a very occasional nature—he always seemed to me to be a trifle strained and uneasy. He longed to smack certain personages on the back,

but he never dared to do it. With women he succeeded a great deal better than with men. Somehow, the men made him either very stiff or very
limp. His bow was wasted upon them and his diffi-
dent attempts at epigram missed fire. I think that
women loved him because he would insist that
everything was "charming" or "exquisite," and because, although he was expected to talk brilliantly,
he really did a great deal of listening. Late in the
proceedings, when the *buffet* had done its harmless,
necessary work, he would open fire and talk amaz-
ingly, and fifteen to twenty women would hang on
his words, doubtless because their hostess had told
them that Mr. Wilde was "so amusing." But the
men hung aloof. When he came away Wilde was
always as eager to know how he had "gone down,"
as a *débutante* is eager to be informed as to the
figure she cut at her first ball. If one said: "You
were great, Oscar," he would glow with honest
pride; if one hummed a little, he would be in the
depths for a week. There were women who didn't
admire him in the least, and some of them were at
no pains to disguise the fact. Long before the
tongue of scandal took definite hold of his name,
there were whispers that there was something
wrong about him; and when Lady Blank referred

to him in his hearing as "that fellow," he became
white with passion and was with difficulty re-
strained from making a demonstration.

On the whole, however, his social evenings were
a source of joy and delight to him, and he would
talk of this or that party for months after it had
taken place, with continual notes of gratification
in his voice. And when, as sometimes happened,
he went to the houses of persons who were not
friends of mine, I could make sure of brilliantly
jewelled accounts of the high jinks and proceedings, and of the honour which had been rendered
to him by brave and fair alike. "Dear Lady
So-and-So," he would say; "Ah! a charming
woman, if you like; came down the staircase to
receive me, for all the world like Œnone coming
down Ida. And the Prime Minister was there, and
I don't mind telling you that he glowered at me.
They hate genius, my boy. And poor old Lord
—— —I have never seen him before—looked to me
like a waiter. Extraordinary that a man of his
position should look so rusty. However, I need
not tell you that he was very civil to me." And
when I asked him what he meant by "rusty," he
said: "Well, he wore such extraordinary clothes."
The real facts of the case doubtless were that his
hostess was not beautiful at all, that the Prime

Minister had not happened to look his way, and
that, despite his rusty suit, old Lord —— had gone
out of his way to meet rather profuse deference
with graciousness.

I don't say that Wilde had no social success,
but what he had was of that curious kind which
is here to-day and forgotten to-morrow, and his
reports of it were always slightly exaggerated. It
was on such a slender basis that he built up the
fabric of wonder and splendour with regard to
"rank" which he afterwards spread out for us in
Reading gaol. Throughout, he draws a great line
between "the poor thieves and outcasts with whom
I now associate" and *people of our rank*—never
"people of our intellect," never "people of our culture." He tells us that in prison he became a great
individualist, and apparently it was in prison that
he became a great aristocrat.

In one passage in the published "De Profundis"
he actually uses the words "I had inherited a noble
name." One need not grudge him these tender illusions, and, in a way, there is something rather
pathetic about them. But their encouragement was
so entirely characteristic of the man that it is
impossible to avoid a reference to them in a truthful
portrait. That Wilde did not happen to be nobly
born is certainly nothing to his discredit; that he

should have persistently pretended to noble birth is, on the other hand, fairly contemptible, especially as in his efforts to live up to the part he had allotted to himself he invariably succeeded in behaving in an eminently unaristocratic manner. He lacked a kind heart just as surely as he lacked a coronet, and Norman blood was as alien to him as simple faith.

CHAPTER IV

I AM not sure that this chapter is headed in quite the way that Oscar Wilde's adherents would like it to be. When he wished to seem particularly important, Wilde was wont to describe himself, not only as a Lord of Language, but as the King of Life. His claims to these magniloquent titles have been suffered to pass unquestioned by his critics, and unassailed even by his enemies. The *coterie* of long-haired persons who weep at the mention of "dear Oscar's" name and hold him up for a saint and a martyr, naturally take pride in his own description of himself, and will no doubt consider it remiss of me to leave out one of them from this chapter heading. The King of Life business has always appeared to me to have been settled at the Old Bailey, and since such a title as the Lord of Language is plainly literary in its bearings, I suppose I am free to discuss it from the literary point of view. And I must state at the outset that I am not concerned to deal with Wilde in other than a reasonable, critical spirit. If his fame and writings

had been left to themselves instead of becoming
the subject of attentions on the part of over-zealous
log-rollers on the one hand and catch-penny scandal-
mongers on the other, Wilde would, in the nature
of things, have attained to his proper position in
literary history and to his proper status as an
author. As it is, I maintain that the current views
about his character and his writings are exaggerated and even preposterous—views very far
ahead of the true facts and, in a large measure,
opposed to what Wilde himself would have wished.
Practically everybody nowadays who writes for
pleasure or for profit about Oscar Fingall O'Flaher-
tie Wills Wilde has taken him for granted as a sort
of literary and artistic aristocrat who had a natural
right to the best of life and for whom all beauty
and delicacy were created. One of the most recent
of his biographers says: "Wilde provides us with
the rare spectacle of a man most of whose powers
are those of a spectator, a connoisseur, a man for
whom pictures are painted and books written, the
perfect elaborator for whom the artist hopes in his
heart." I have never seen a fault of taste, a fault
of judgment or a fault of intellect attributed to
him. Even his vices are held up to us as having
been necessary to the development of his chartered
and immaculate soul, and as having contributed

and been necessary to the perfection of his work. Greater bunkum was never propagated. Wilde was far from being in any sense a perfervid worshipper of the beautiful. To suggest that beauty was all in all for him is to suggest what is not true. He was never content that other people should write fine poetry or fine prose for him to admire, his sole ambition being to write fine things himself—not especially for the fine thing's sake, but for the sake of being able to pose as the one great and superior person in all the world. It is not to Wilde's discredit, perhaps, that he praised but little or, as one might say, frugally. There was nobody of his time who greatly required to be praised. He professed the stock admiration for Tennyson, Swinburne, Meredith and Pater; but when he expressed it— which was seldom—it was always with the reservation that of the five he himself was the greatest. There were occasions, of course, when he could be adulatory, and even obsequious; but this was either to dead men or to those of his contemporaries who were engaged in arts with which he was not concerned as a practitioner. His sonnets to Miss Ellen Terry and the late Henry Irving may stand for his monument in this special line. As to artists painting pictures for him, and so forth, the great quarrel of his life was with Whistler, from whom he de-

rived practically everything that he affected to
know about art and whose work he believed to be
"vastly overrated." Of pictures in their relation
to beauty he had little or no appreciation. Just as
the far-famed blue china at Oxford was valuable
to him because he could make *mots* over it and get
himself talked about, so all his views and his expressions of opinion with respect to art were not
the views and opinions of the person who loves and
knows art, but were designed to illustrate his own
singularity or superiority, or to support a pose. In
spite of all he wrote and said on the subject, and in
spite of all that has been said and written by his
admirers, there is nothing of Wilde that persists
in criticism on the art side which is not to be found
in Whistler's "Ten o'clock," or which he had not
gleaned either from his contemporaries or from
the older writers on the literary side. In order
to show more clearly what I mean, let us take the
preface to "Dorian Gray," which, as is well known,
consists of a number of aphorisms concerning art
and criticism as Wilde is supposed to have believed
in them. I quote some of them:—

The artist is the creator of beautiful things.

To reveal art and conceal the artist is art's
aim.

The critic is he who can translate into another manner or a new material his impression of beautiful things.

The highest, as the lowest, form of criticism is a mode of autobiography.

Those who find ugly meanings in beautiful things are corrupt without being charming. This is a fault.

Those who find beautiful meanings in beautiful things are the cultivated. For these there is hope.

They are the elect to whom beautiful things mean only beauty.

There is no such thing as a moral or an immoral book. Books are well written or badly written. That is all.

The nineteenth-century dislike of realism is the rage of Caliban seeing his own face in a glass.

The nineteenth-century dislike of romanticism is the rage of Caliban not seeing his own face in a glass.

The moral life of man forms part of the subject-matter of the artist, but the morality of art consists in the perfect use of an imperfect medium.

No artist desires to prove anything. Even things that are true can be proved.

Thought and language are to the artist instruments of an art.

Vice and virtue are to the artist materials for an art.

From the point of view of form, the type of all the arts is the art of the musician. From the point of view of feeling, the actor's craft is the type.

It is the spectator and not life that art really mirrors.

Diversity of opinion about a work of art shows that the work is new, complex and vital.

When critics disagree the artist is in accord with himself.

We can forgive a man for making a useful thing as long as he does not admire it. The only excuse for making a useless thing is that one admires it intensely.

All art is quite useless.

These remarks have been held up to us as Wilde's *credo,* and slight and few though they be, it is the fact that they do really epitomise what some people call his "teaching." One has only to glance at them, however, to perceive that without exception they are either obvious or perverted truisms or the merest glosses on quite hoary critical adages. For example, "The artist is the creator of beautiful things" must have been said at least a thousand times before Wilde suddenly rushed upon the world with it as a new and marvellous discovery. "To reveal art and conceal the artist is art's aim" is a very cheap variant of the saying that language was invented to conceal one's thoughts, or Horace's old tag: *"Ars est celare artem."* "The highest and lowest form of criticism is a form of autobiography" is merely to say what was said by Rousseau —namely: that all writing is in essence autobiographical; while "It is the spectator and not life, that art really mirrors" is merely Shakespeare's "Beauty is in the eye of the beholder," clumsily rendered. All the talk about there being no such thing as a moral or an immoral book, and about art being quite useless, is the merest perversion and fiddle-de-dee, as anybody who is not in the last stage of idiocy will perceive for himself.

I maintain that this statement of Wilde—which, by the way, did not originally appear as a preface to "Dorian Gray," but was painfully and carefully compiled when its author was at the height of his achievement and wished to pontificate—shows us clearly the nature of the man's mind, which was a shallow and comparatively feeble mind, incapable of grappling unaided with even moderately profound things, and disposed to fribble and antic with old thoughts for lack of power to evolve new ones. It was a mind which was continually discovering with a glow that two and two make four, or pretending to discover with a much warmer glow that two and two make five. In every scrap that he wrote, leaving out, of course, the poems, you will find this feeble, mediocre, but, withal, vain-glorious instrument hard at work on the fearful business of saying nothing in such a way that foolish people will shout about it.

Wilde knew himself for a shallow and oblique thinker. The fact that he never did anything really great has been set down to his indolence. It was due really to shallowness rather than indolence. When he found that nobody would read his poetry, he became most indolent about the writing of verses and complained that there was nothing for a poet of his eminence to write about. When he found that people would listen to lectures written on a basis of Whistler and William Morris, he wrote and delivered such lectures with an industry worthy of the best of causes. And when he found actor-managers who would produce money "on account" for such drama as "Lady Windermere's Fan" and such comedy as "The Importance of being Earnest," he wrote plays till the sweat fairly rolled off him. But he was conscious, as every unbiassed contemporary critic was conscious, that he ran very far short of the achievement of which he was wont to plume himself, and he knew that when it came to serious things he was always considered more or less of a dabbler.

Like most Irishmen, he was troubled all his life with attacks of regret which he was accustomed to call remorse. He believed that he had supreme gifts and that he had squandered them; he never could see that it was impossible that a man who pretended, as he pretended, could ever have had supreme gifts. His remorse over the squandering of these alleged gifts was at times ludicrous to behold. He would bemoan his wasted life and come very nigh shedding tears about his shallowness at two o'clock in the morning; while at one o'clock the same day he would be swallowing ortolans as if they were oysters and swearing over some silly liqueur that he was the greatest genius that ever lived.

In time, this notion of shallowness became an obsession with him. He makes constant use of the word "shallow" in his writings, and right through "De Profundis" you find him crying "the supreme

vice is shallowness," in and out of season, and without the remotest reference to the context. Of
course, if we endeavour to look into the psychology
of the situation, we perceive clearly that it was impossible for a man of Wilde's type to do any really
big work, and he certainly never did do it. His
claims to be considered as a "Lord of Language"
will not bear looking into. He wrote passable verse
and competent prose, but he wrote no better verse
and no better prose than several other men of his
time whose writings are more or less forgotten.
We have it on the statement of Mr. Justice Darling
that Wilde could "conjure with words." I should
like chapter and verse for any verbal conjuring
which can be considered worth remembering, or
which, for that matter, is remembered. I think
that all Wilde did for the English language was to
degrade, abuse or make ridiculous such words as
"exquisite," "wonderful," "charming," "delightful," "delicate," and so forth. He bored me to
death at times with his "How perfectly wonderful
of you!" while his "charming fellows" and "charming ladies," "delicious dishes," "exquisite liqueurs"
and general ecstatics were like sands on the sea
where the blue wave rolls nightly. He was plagued
with the Irishman's propensity to muddle his
"shalls" and "wills," and I found in him an utter

incapacity to understand or appreciate, in the literary sense, certain plain English idioms with which any man possessed of a feeling for language would never have had the slightest trouble. I remember having a lengthy and fearful argument with him over Shakespeare's use of the word "your" in such phrases as "your tanner will last you eleven years." He could understand neither the force nor the sense of such usages and, though he "tumbled" in the end, he was a fearful time about it. One does not expect such dullness in a Lord of Language.

CHAPTER V

ACCORDING to the Ransome book—the biographical details in which, its author admits, have been checked by Mr. Robert Ross—Oscar Wilde was the son of William Wilde, "knighted in 1864, a celebrated oculist and aurist, a man of great intellectuality and uncertain temper, a runner after girls, with a lusty enjoyment of life, and a delight in falling stars and thunderstorms."

This is an ingenious way of presenting a decidedly dubious and unpleasing character to an awe-stricken world. Wilde's father was certainly a knight; but heaven alone knows who his grandfather was. It is also to be noted that while Sir William Wilde may have died "a celebrated oculist and aurist," he began life as an apothecary, and for years kept a chemist's shop in an obscure part of Dublin. The "runner after girls" admission on the part of Messrs. Ransome and Ross is also very touching, seeing that William Wilde had once been prosecuted for insulting a lady patient and that everybody knows the story of Wilde's father and the witty veterinary surgeon who rallied him on the subject with one of the sharpest bits of sarcasm that ever fell from a man's mouth.

It is perhaps necessary for me to say here that I have never in my life laid any great stress upon the advantages of birth. If a man's manners and disposition are all right, I am not greatly concerned to know that his father drove pigs or got locked up for stealing spoons. At the same time, I have never been able to repress feelings of amused contempt for that numerous body of persons who, having no ancestry or forbears to speak of, make a point of proclaiming themselves to be persons of family, and invent all manner of legends to support their supposed exalted birth.

In the case of Wilde, it is due to him to say that he kept his parentage and extraction fairly in the background so far as I was concerned. He admitted that he belonged to the Irish middle classes and prided himself on having risen to academic honour, not with the help of money, but by sheer force of intellect. This was in the early days of our acquaintance. Ultimately, when he had managed to get out of the rut of bohemianism and to find his way into respectable society, he began to conceive himself in the light of a very great social figure, and it was easy for him to suppose that he was a born member of the aristocracy and that all his people belonged to what Burke, I believe, calls "The titled landed and official classes." I used to smile at these pretensions and joke with him about them; and he would admit that he was foolish. But the fact remains that to the end of his life he kept up the legend of his high birth and connections, and was eager always to pass himself off as a great gentleman.

His biographers have taken up the wondrous tale and, without saying so in as many words, they lead the polite world of Wilde worshippers to believe that their saint was what the young lady called "a gentleman in his own right." The Wildes "were people of consideration in Dublin," says the zealous Mr. Ransome: "his school-fellows did not have to ask Wilde who his father was." Well, possibly they didn't—for very different reasons than those Mr. Ransome would have us conjure up. Down to the time of my first meeting Wilde, he had never had any real footing in society and, though he fought for it desperately during the period of our friendship, I doubt if he ever really got it. He was too obviously the tuft-hunter and the snob ever to be liked by the people for whose acquaintance he sighed. I never could see why a man of his talents and mode of life should have been so desperately anxious to be "hail fellow well met" with some of the dullest and silliest people in the world; but there can be no doubt that he dearly loved a lord and would put up with a great deal of pain and inconvenience on the mere chance of a casual word or two with a duchess. When our acquaintance began he knew nobody, and, though his name was in the papers and his picture turned up from time to time in *Punch,* you never saw him at the places where he would have given his soul to be. He told me that at Magdalen he had managed to get on terms with an unmarried duke, but before this beam of sunshine had shone upon him for a year or two, the duke incontinently married and the duchess intervened and put an end to the intimacy.

Wilde's own set of friends and acquaintances struck one as being a peculiar assemblage; but he assured me that they were great and charming people and that they were all on the high road to eminence and fame; and, being young and unversed in the world's ways, I took him at his word and set down my incapacity to appreciate his immediate *entourage* to my own dullness and lack of perspicacity. The first stars in the firmament of charming fellows and world-compelling geniuses brought to me by Wilde were Mr. Robert Ross and Mr.

CARICATURE BY MAX BEERBOHM OF OSCAR WILDE AND
LORD ALFRED DOUGLAS

Reggie Turner. According to the allegations brought against me at the Ransome trial, when Wilde entertained these gentlemen at dinner he did it in Soho and with the help of a shilling bottle of Medoc; whereas when I, Lord Alfred Douglas, was his guest, it was always at Willis's rooms and to the accompaniment of specially imported *patés* from Strasbourg and priceless champagnes. In point of fact, all four of us drank a good many humble whiskies and sodas at the Café Royal and dined and lunched at the same place without any great effusions of money on anybody's part. Wilde was a doughty and assiduous trencherman. I would have backed him to eat the head off a brewer's dray-man three times a day, and his capacity for whisky and soda knew no bounds. The marvel of it was that he never became really drunk, though from four o'clock in the afternoon till three in the morning he was never really sober. The more he drank the more he talked, and without whisky he could neither talk nor write.

After Messrs. Ross and Turner, Wilde brought along the late Ernest Dowson, who, for some reason or other, seemed scared out of his wits; Mr. Max Beerbohm, who giggled prettily at everything either Wilde or I said; and Mr. Frank Harris, who wore the same costly furs and roared in the same sucking-dove way as still continues to delight his troops of friends. They were a merry and, I am afraid, a rather careless company. They talked art, poetry and politics; none of them seemed to have much to do, though I believe all of them were fairly busy men and, on the whole, they were pleasant enough people to meet.

Gradually, however, the acquaintance between myself and Wilde began to strengthen and become more intimate. I took him to my mother's place near Ascot and introduced him to a good many people whom he considered to be important. He met my cousin, George Wyndham, who, I believe, asked him down afterwards to Clouds, and, at his very special request, I introduced him to my brother, Viscount Drumlanrig, at that time a Lord-in-Waiting to Queen Victoria. No two men could have less in common than Drumlanrig and Wilde. On one hand you had a soldier and a sportsman, with perhaps a bit of the courtier thrown in; on the other hand you had the overdressed Bohemian, with his hair nicely parted and very anxious to be friendly and charming. My brother was amused and, though they did not meet more than three times, it was years before Wilde ceased to talk pompously of "my friend, Lord Drumlanrig, Lord-in-Waiting to Her Majesty." I also introduced him to my grandfather, Mr. Alfred Montgomery, who took a violent and invincible dislike to him and declined to meet him again.

In addition to the people I have mentioned, Wilde always had on hand a sort of job line of weird and wonderful acquaintances whose names were for ever on his lips and whose possessions—intellectual and otherwise—were supposed to be fabulous. He would come a few minutes late for lunch and beg to be excused for unpunctuality. "The fact of the matter is," he would say, "I have spent a most delightful morning with my dear friend, Mr. Balsam Bassy—a charming fellow with a face like a Michel Angelo drawing and a mind like Benvenuto Cellini. I would have brought him in to lunch—he is dying to make your acquaintance—but he has to go down to his uncle's place in Devonshire and couldn't miss the two-fifty on any account." There would follow a long and highly elaborate statement of Mr. Balsam Bassy's many gifts, graces and accomplishments, his wonderful powers of conversation, the exquisite *mots* he perpetrated, and the charming poetry that he could write if he would only take the trouble to live his own life instead of frivolling it away in the highest circles. Wilde had, to my knowledge, at least half a dozen "Balsam Bassys" going at one time and, though I only saw one of them in the flesh, I believe they were real persons, and that Wilde believed all he had invented about them. The solitary "Balsam Bassy" he produced on an occasion when he could not help himself, as the man sailed right into us at supper, turned out to be a very mild and inoffensive gentleman who possessed an allowance of two hundred and fifty pounds a year from his uncle, a brewer, but with no more talent—let alone genius—than a box of matches. When I observed to Wilde that this particular Mr. Balsam Bassy did not seem quite to come up to expectations, he became very angry and said that the fact that Mr. Balsam Bassy was his friend was a sufficient passport for him to any society. I said that I thought it was, and there the matter dropped.

The large number of persons of eminence whom Wilde knew in a casual way would, of course, make a long list, but of his friends and intimates—the people who, so to say, gyrated immediately around him—I have given a full account. It should be added that Wilde knew Beardsley, whom he was disposed to patronise, and Mr. George Bernard Shaw, who was then a writer on the *Star*. Of Shaw he had a high opinion and prophesied for him a future in a walk of life far other than the one in which he has succeeded. Probably if he had never known Shaw he would never have written the "Soul of Man." While Shaw's socialism was a very much redder and more blatant affair in those days than it is now, it attracted Wilde because it was odd and Shaw was Irish. Though a mild Liberal by pretension, Wilde was always a rebel in his heart. "Down with everything that's up and up with everything that's down" was his intellectual motto. If he had not met Shaw he would probably have kept his views about the social order of things to himself. Shaw helped him to a species of socialism which looks very revolutionary but which is really designed to benefit the rich rather than the poor. Like pretty well everything else that Wilde wrote, "The Soul of Man under Socialism" fails entirely when you come to look into it. It is neither fish, flesh, fowl nor good red herring, and its main argument—namely, that human beings will never be happy till they have got rid of altruism—is, of course, the obvious reverse of the truth.

It may be that the account I have given of Wilde's circle will come with a shock of disappointment to those who have been accustomed to the Ross-Ransome-Sherard versions as to his mode of life. The absence of distinguished names is certainly conspicuous. But as I am writing the truth and not a fairy story, I am compelled to stick to the

actual facts, which are that Wilde, during all the
time I knew him, was not on terms of anything like
intimacy with any of the distinguished people of
his day. He was continually talking of his various
eminent contemporaries as if he were on terms of
friendship with them; he constantly referred to
Edward Burne-Jones, to William Morris, to Ruskin,
to Meredith, to Tennyson, Swinburne, Browning
and the rest; and he referred to them always as if
he had at one time been most friendly with them.
Whether this were or were not the case I have no
means of settling authoritatively: I can only speak
of the period of his life during which I knew him
and was continually in his society—namely, from
the year 1892 to the time of his death—and I say
positively that during the whole of that time he
never had the slightest intercourse with any of the
persons mentioned. I believe Wilde had at one time
a slight acquaintance with Burne-Jones; but on two
occasions when I myself met the latter at Clouds,
the country house of my uncle, the late Mr. Percy
Wyndham, I never heard him mention Wilde's
name. I believe he knew Ruskin at Oxford, but
only in the way in which any undergraduate could
know him if he wished to do so. Browning he had
met once or twice, and the same applies to Meredith.
I do not believe that he ever saw or, at any rate,

spoke either to Tennyson or Swinburne. Yet to hear him talk of all these people one would have supposed that he was a regular member of their circle. When I was with Wilde, before his downfall and imprisonment I accepted all he told me as to his friendship with the intellectual giants of his time as gospel truth, and it was not till long afterwards that it struck me as curious that we never came across any of these celebrities; that Wilde was never able to get one of them to come to his house, and never by any chance went to see them at theirs.

A good example of Wilde's pushfulness in this line of pretended intimacy with celebrated people is furnished by the terms of his dedication of one of his plays: "To the dear memory of Robert, Earl of Lytton." I have it on the authority of Mr. Neville Lytton, the younger son of the late Lord Lytton, that his father scarcely knew Wilde, and had only met him on one or two occasions, and that he might or might not have been flattered by Wilde's dedication. The same applies to his supposed French acquaintance. According to Wilde's own account, he knew everybody in France who was worth knowing, but, as a fact, he had only the very slightest knowledge of a few of them, derived from meeting them once or twice at luncheon or dinner-parties at the time he wrote his play "Salome." This question is settled by the articles which have appeared on the subject in France by M. Henri de Régnier and the Vicomte d'Humières.

After he left prison, of course nobody knew him, but at the very height of his fame and success the facts were as I have stated. The same applies to social as opposed to literary and artistic lights. When I was twenty-three years of age I was elected to an institution called the Crabbet Club, which had been founded by my cousin, Mr. Wilfrid Blunt. The club met once a year at Mr. Wilfrid Blunt's country house, Crabbet Park, for the purpose of playing lawn-tennis and reading poems composed by the members of the club for a prize. Among the members of the club were George Curzon—now Lord Curzon of Kedlestone—George Wyndham, George Leveson-Gower—then Comptroller of the Queen's Household: the "Trinity of Georges," as some one called them in a prize poem; Lord Houghton, now Lord Crewe, Mr. Harry Cust, Mr. Godfrey Webb, Mr. Mark Napier, the late Lord Cairns, Mr. "Lulu" Harcourt and a lot more. Mr. Blunt had made Oscar Wilde a member of this club, and Wilde attended one meeting. It was the custom that any new member should be proposed in a speech at dinner on the first night of the meeting and opposed by some one else. Wilde was opposed by George Curzon, who attacked him in a brilliant, humorous, witty but deadly speech in such a very scathing way that he never could be induced to go to another meeting of the Club. As an undoubted member of this club he certainly could claim to know the other members, and he actually passed one *Saturday to Monday* at Crabbet in their company. He never forgot it, and never forgot to refer to them by their Christian names ever afterwards; but none of them ever came to Wilde's house or asked him to his, with the solitary exception of George Wyndham, under circumstances which I have already detailed. On the only occasion on which I attended a meeting of the Crabbet Club I was proposed by George Wyndham and opposed in a friendly way by Hubert Howard, who was afterwards killed at the battle of Omdurman. The Crabbet Club was only a club in name. There was no subscription and no entrance fee, and admittance to it was simply by invitation of Mr. Blunt, who used the annual occasion of the meeting of the club as a pretext for a charming and most lavish hospitality. I was actually the last member to join it, and the year I joined was the last year of its existence. One of the rules of the club was that Prime Ministers, Bishops, and Viceroys were not eligible for membership, and that any member found guilty of attaining such positions should be at once expelled. Nothing was said about convicts, but when two of the members (Lord Curzon and Lord Houghton) became Viceroys, and one (Oscar Wilde) was sent to prison, Mr. Blunt came to the conclusion that the Crabbet Club had better be wound up; and it lives now only as a glorious memory and by virtue of a privately printed volume of prize and other poems, mostly of a satirical nature, which would make the fortune of a dealer in rare books if he could get hold of a copy. I may be excused for mentioning with pride that I won the lawn-tennis tournament of my year, and divided the honours of the Prize Poem with the late Mr. Godfrey Webb, known as "Webber" to his numerous friends. To be strictly accurate, Mr. Godfrey Webb was declared the laureate of the year, and invested with the laurel wreath, while a special prize was awarded to me for my poem. It was a beautifully bound edition of Surrey's and Wyatt's sonnets, and I regret to say that I left it behind me at Naples, along with a great many other valuable and interesting books, in the charge of Oscar Wilde when I handed over my villa to him. All these books Wilde sold or lost soon after I left Naples.

The prize for the Lawn Tennis Tournament I still have in my possession. It is a handsome silver cup of the Georgian period, and is inscribed as follows:

"In Youth and Crabbed Age."
Crabbet Club,
1894.

CHAPTER VI

IN 1895 my friendship with Oscar Wilde had ripened into an intimacy which was an affair for the gossips. We were inseparable: wherever Wilde went I went, and wherever I went Wilde went. I was living at my mother's house in Cadogan Place, and Wilde at his house in Tite Street. We lunched and dined usually at the Café Royal or at the Savoy; we visited the theatres and music-halls of an evening, and we often wound up the day with supper at Willis's rooms. I had left Oxford and my time was my own. Money did not trouble me much in those days. My father allowed me three hundred and fifty pounds a year for pocket money; the necessaries and luxuries of life were always at my disposal at home and in the houses of my numerous friends and relatives; and whenever I wanted money I had merely to ask my mother or my indulgent Grandfather Montgomery for it. One way or another, I dare say I was living at the rate of at least fifteen hundred a

OSCAR WILDE'S HOUSE, 16 TITE STREET, CHELSEA

year. Wilde was an expensive sort of friend, particularly after he began to consider himself a
gourmet and a man of the great world. He gave
fairly expensive entertainments, and although a
chop and a pint of bitter beer at some respectable
inn would always have done for me, I never professed to be insensible to the charms of good cooking, and when it came to ordering and paying for
a dinner for my friends I was certainly not to be
outdone by Wilde. At the Ransome trial, among
the charges brought against me on the strength
of the precious document which Mr. Ross has
handed to the British Museum, was that of extrava-
gance, in respect of which I had to meet Wilde's
stories of the long-departed menus of some of our
Lucullian feasts. It was suggested that we lived
on nothing but "delicious ortolans"—by the way,
are there any ortolans that are not delicious?—and
foie gras from Strasbourg, which we made a point
of washing down with Perrier Jouet and topped
off with fifty-year-old brandy. Of course, I do not
profess to remember what I had for dinner twenty
years ago; but any man about town knows that one
can dine very comfortably for a sovereign, and I
happen to remember that Wilde always considered
a sovereign quite a good deal of money. It was
further suggested that between the autumn of 1892

and the date of his imprisonment—that is to say, in
less than three years—Wilde spent with me and on
me more than five thousand pounds in actual money,
irrespective of the bills he incurred. But in plain
terms this means that he spent at least forty pounds
a week in entertaining me. So that for three years
I must have been eating three meals a day and
twenty-one meals a week, at a cost and charge of
two pounds a meal, with Oscar Wilde. I cannot
have disbursed a penny on myself or on him and, at
the end of the three years, I ought to have had a
thousand or two in the bank and a stone or two of
flesh to spare. In point of fact, even in those early
days I spent a great deal more money on Wilde than
he spent on me, and my weight has stood at less
than ten stone five ever since I can remember, which,
for a man of my height, does not point to much
gourmandising. It is a pretty thing that any
gentleman should be compelled to go into such matters, but as the world has already been told and
is to be told again in 1960 that I got through five
thousand pounds' worth of Wilde's ortolans and
Perrier Jouet in three years, I here and now venture
to tell the world that I did nothing of the kind. In
the three years in question, it is exceedingly doubt-
ful whether Wilde ever had five thousand pounds
at his disposal. He had developed expensive tastes

in many other directions besides food and drink:
he dressed expensively, he wore expensive jewellery, he made presents of jewellery and money to
all sorts of ridiculous people; the upkeep of his
house in Tite Street must have run him into at
least a thousand a year; he travelled a good deal
and made expensive stays in Paris, at Homburg
and in Italy; and, not to put too fine a point on it,
he was continually short of money.   On several
occasions I borrowed money from moneylenders
at his suggestion and instigation, and he invariably
helped himself liberally, not only to these sums but
to sums of money which I obtained from my mother
and from my other relatives.   Indeed, so far as my
money was concerned, we had a common purse.   It
never occurred to me to refuse him anything.
Nothing was too good for him, and I always regarded him as a man who, although he might have
spurts of money, was without proper income and
resources, and was consequently to be helped out
whenever occasion demanded.   To take an instance
in point: just before "The Woman of no Importance" was put on at the Haymarket I went to a
moneylender and borrowed two hundred and fifty
pounds.   At lunch I showed Wilde the money in ten-
pound notes, and he took them into his hand and said:
"How beautiful they are and how wonderful it is of

you to be able to get them." Then, with a laugh, he put five or six of them into his own pocket and handed me the balance. I thought no more about it at the moment than I should have thought of sharing a bottle of wine with him. Indeed, I got the money with the intention of giving him some of it because he had been groaning for over a week about his hard-upness. This is only one instance of many. All my life I have been free-handed and careless about money. I was well over thirty years of age before it dawned upon me that money did not grow on the trees on the family estate. There are plenty of people who are now living who know me well, and I should like to hear one of them who would tell me that I am "thrifty" or that I permit my friends to pay out of their turn. It is true that Wilde and I were for a long period on terms of friendship which were quite outside and beyond the "you-ask-me-to-dinner-and-I-ask-you-back-again" principle; but it is grotesquely untrue to suggest that he wasted any appreciable part of his substance upon me. Wilde had a great way of making everything appear important. He was very fond of sending for the managers of restaurants to consult them over the merits of wine or to bid them summon the chef to receive instruction or compliment, as the case might be. These were not practices of mine, and never have been. Up to the time of my meeting Oscar Wilde, I had been accustomed to live at great houses, and the best food and the best drink were the only sort I knew about. It never occurred to me that Wilde's "exquisite" spreads were anything out of the ordinary. I suppose the cooking at the Café Royal or at the Savoy Hotel is good, but it is certainly, to say the least, no better than what one gets in a good house or at a good club. Wilde made fusses and went through elaborate rituals over the ordering of his meals. I, for my part, ordered, ate and paid for them, and thought nothing further about it.

As I have said, our constant appearances together at cafés, restaurants, theatres and public places set the gossips wagging their tongues. I heard all sorts of rumours which were silly on the face of them and which were a good deal sillier when one thought about them. Naturally, I ignored them utterly. I am convinced that some of the whispers and hints that went around were set going by persons who deemed that I had supplanted them in Wilde's good graces and who were annoyed because, while he still continued to know them, he ceased, in a great measure, to frequent their company. In any case, I was made to feel that certain people were very sore about my

"monopolising Wilde." Egged on doubtless by
what she heard, even Mrs. Wilde—with whom I
always had been on the most friendly terms—
began to say that I took up a great deal too much
of Oscar's time, and Wilde once told me that she
had made difficulties about our being so much together. I told him that we certainly did seem to
be always together, and I offered to go away and
leave him to his own devices; but he said that
this would be unbearable to him and that he had
made Mrs. Wilde understand and that he had mentioned the matter to me in the idlest way and without any notion that I should be so foolish as to take
him seriously. So our lives drifted along as usual.
I may here mention that for the first three years
of my close intimacy with Oscar Wilde I never
heard a coarse or indelicate allusion come out of
his mouth. I knew him for a somewhat cynical and
insincere kind of humourist; I was not blind to his
faults of vanity and his occasional lapses into vulgar manners; I knew he was no saint, even as men
of the world go; but I considered that he was a
man of decent life, and I never heard from him a
word or a sign which made me think otherwise.
He treated me always with the greatest and, I may
even say, the most elaborate courtesy, and I noticed
particularly that when we were in the society of

men who were apt to kick somewhat over the traces and indulge in Rabelaisian conversation Wilde was eagerly careful to turn or suppress the talk. He therefore seemed to be all that a man should be; and when I heard on one or two occasions certain other hints of tendencies of his, I repudiated them with indignation, believing that, as I was his close friend, I knew him through and through, and feeling that there could not possibly be any truth in what was suggested.

Some years before I met Wilde my mother had found it desirable to divorce my father, and at the time to which I am now referring the family relationships were not exactly running smooth. To be quite frank, I had conceived feelings of resentment against my father on account of his treatment of my mother which I am afraid were far from filial. You may judge, then, of my anger when Wilde one day told me that Lord Queensberry had sent him a letter in which he requested Wilde to terminate his friendship with me at once, inasmuch as he did not think it would be beneficial to me. Wilde asked me what he should do, and I told him to take no notice of the letter. Later, my father sent me a letter in which he told me what he had said to Wilde, and threatened to cut off my allowance if I did not at once terminate the acquaintance.

I was not aware of any grounds upon which Lord Queensberry could make such a request, and concluded that he had written to me for the mere purpose of annoyance and because he knew that I had taken sides with my mother since the divorce proceedings. Consequently, I sent him a fairly stinging reply, and a heated correspondence followed. Portions of that correspondence have been preserved in glass cases by careful lawyers, and these relics of an unpleasant feud have been brought up against me in various cross-examinations with a view to proving that I was an unfilial brute and that I treated my own father very badly.

In the light of what has happened since, I know that I was hasty and mistaken, but one cannot be the son of the eighth Marquis of Queensberry nor a member of the family of Douglas without having the defects of one's qualities. I did not sit down to the abuse of my father in the manner of a person without spirit for the very simple reason that I am not devoid of spirit and never shall be. However, before he died my father sent for me and there was a complete reconciliation between us, and he left me every shilling that could possibly be arranged for me out of his very considerable estate.

Failing to make disruption between myself and Wilde, Lord Queensberry adopted a different line

STATION:- SEMLEY.
TELEGRAMS:- EAST KNOYLE.

CLOUDS.
EAST KNOYLE,
SALISBURY.

25. iv. 1913

My dear Bosie
          Your letter made me
rejoice, not that I needed
anything to shew that
you have a kind heart
as well as a brave one.
You have been through a
furnace of affliction &,

when that happens to a
man, it is good to see
his true ~~self~~ nature
reasserting itself at once.
You may rest assured that
all your friends think the
hidden attack made on you
a base thing. several
have spoken to me to that
effect & none in any other
                              way).
        ever yr affecte cousin
          Geo Wyndham

of tactics; and, I believe, with the sincere view of saving me from what he knew was an undesirable entanglement, he went ahead to disgrace Wilde publicly. At a theatre where one of Wilde's plays was running he caused a bouquet of carrots to be handed up to Wilde over the footlights, and he left his card on him at his club with certain odious remarks written on the back of it. I need scarcely say that Wilde was very much distressed. He came to me in a great state about it and said that it was most wicked and cruel of my father to treat him in this way and that, unless an immediate apology was forthcoming, he would have no alternative but to prosecute Lord Queensberry for criminal libel. I was a little bit nettled at the tone he took, as he seemed to imply by his air that I was in some way to blame for what had happened; and I said at once: "You are not in the least likely to get apologies from my father and, so far as I am concerned, you can prosecute and be blowed!"

It has been widely asserted that I went out of my way to instigate these proceedings against my father. It is quite certain that I did not go on my bended knees to ask Wilde not to take proceedings. He assured me that the suggestions and accusation against him were quite false and without foundation. I had not the smallest reason to sup-

pose that he was lying to me, and I undoubtedly
allowed matters to take their course. I will go
further, and say that in a sense I was not sorry
that Lord Queensberry should be brought to book
for what I considered to be his very bad treatment
of both myself and Wilde. I went with Wilde, at
his request, to see a lawyer on the subject. This
lawyer had been recommended to him by Robert
Ross, who also accompanied us on this occasion.
He advised proceedings, and we went to Bow Street
and procured a warrant for my father's arrest. On
the morning the warrant was executed Wilde came
to me in a condition bordering on hysteria, told
me that he had no money and that at least three
hundred pounds were required in order that the
case might go on. At his urgent solicitation, I
gave him three hundred and sixty pounds to give
to his solicitor. (The figures appear in my bank-
book and were proved at the Ransome trial.) This,
I am told, was most unnatural conduct. Wilde, for
his part, pointed out that it was entirely through his
friendship for me that he had to suffer Lord
Queensberry's insults, and that unless he went on
with the prosecution he would be branded throughout Europe for a person of vicious and abominable
life; and that, as I had been the means of getting
him into the trouble, it would be a poor thing if

I would not find a few hundreds to get him out again. What was I to do—and what would any man so placed have done? I should have liked to have quoted verbatim Wilde's version of this episode as it was put to me at the Ransome trial; but since the manuscript of this book was completed Mr. Robert Ross has obtained an injunction against me, by which I am precluded from quoting any part of the unpublished "De Profundis" manuscript. This unpublished part has been used against me in the most frightful manner. Venomous passages have been read in open court and reproduced in hundreds of newspapers, and yet I understand I am debarred from quoting from it for the purpose of replying to it and pointing out its obvious falsity. It is unnecessary for me to enlarge on the absolute negation of every principle of justice and common sense which is involved in such a decision: it is too obvious for that. I do not say that such decision may not be a correct interpretation of the law as it exists, though it is hard to believe it. What I do say is that the existence of such a law is a disgrace and a danger to the community, for it is obvious that under its provisions any man can foully slander another and so arrange his slander that reply to it becomes impossible during the lifetime of the slandered. For example, there is nothing to prevent

me from writing a long letter, say, to Mr. Justice
Astbury—the judge who granted Mr. Ross the
interim injunction restraining me from quoting
passages from the unpublished "De Profundis." I
can, if I please, accuse him in this letter of every
sort of crime and impute to him every kind of base-
ness; I can attack his parents and his relations and
I can ascribe to him imaginary words alleged to
have been spoken by him, and I can invent imaginary scenes in which I allege that he has taken
part. All I have to do is to hand this letter to a
friend and give him instructions that after my
death it is to be placed in the British Museum and
kept there till such time as the friend may think
fitting to bring it out and publish it. If Mr. Justice
Astbury should happen to outlive me, and if he
should thereupon by some chance get knowledge of
the fact that a long epistle addressed to him and
containing a violent attack on his character is lying
in the British Museum and is to be published in fifty
years' time, he will be powerless to take the smallest
step to prevent the publication of this posthumous
libel, and he will not even be able to defend himself
against the accusations it contains. The copyright
in the manuscript will be the property of my heirs
and executors, and should Mr. Justice Astbury
propose to quote any part of it with a view to show-

ing its scandalous and ridiculous falsity he will immediately be pulled up by the law of copyright. My slanderous and shameful letter will be a valuable literary property; for Mr. Justice Astbury to quote passages from it would be injurious to its market value. In vain he would protest that he was surely entitled to defend himself against an attack made on him by a dead man and designed to be made public to the world after his own death. He would simply be told that "the law is quite clear," and he would have to grin and bear it as well as he could, just as I have to do under precisely similar circumstances. What I can, at any rate, legitimately do—even within the narrow compass which Mr. Justice Astbury's interpretation of the law allows me—is to set out the true facts connected with this period of Wilde's career and my own connection with it.

I desire firstly to state emphatically that I did not force Wilde into taking proceedings against my father. The matter can be summed up in a few sentences. My father had accused Wilde of certain abominations. These accusations it seems were true. Wilde denied the truth of them to me and proceeded to take up what, in view of the facts known to himself and not to me, was a ridiculous prosecution against my father. He was, of course, beaten, and the authorities turned upon him and convicted him of crimes which he had denied. Then I became a convenient scapegoat.

I did *not* drag Wilde down to Bow Street to procure a warrant. I went with him, but at his own request. The suggestion of coercion—either moral or physical—is ridiculous. Here was the "King of Life"—a great big, fat, strong fellow, full of brains and forty-one years of age—"in the prime of his splendid manhood," as one of his admirers puts it; and I was sixteen years his junior —that is to say, twenty-four years of age. The real fact is that he had something inside him that I knew nothing about—namely and to wit, a guilty conscience. He was too much of a coward to tell me that he was guilty of the charges the Marquis of Queensberry had levelled at him, and he was too much of a coward, even, to go to Bow Street for a warrant alone: so he came whimpering to me to go with him.

I did *not* coerce or cajole Wilde into going to Monte Carlo at this time, nor did Wilde pay my expenses or my gambling losses. Wilde said his nerves were all broken up. He had never been to Monte Carlo, and we went there in order that he might be distracted from the question of the trial, upon which he seemed to brood a great deal.

THE LATE MARQUIS OF QUEENSBERRY

Believing him to be an innocent man, I told him
that he was a fool to worry and that it was the other
side who ought to do the worrying, and we went to
Monte Carlo. I have frequently been to Monte
Carlo, and I have never in my life spent more than
two hours at a stretch in the rooms. On this particular occasion I was less frequently in the rooms
and for less periods of time than I have ever been
before or since, largely because Wilde was with me.
More often than not he was with me in the rooms,
and I gave him more than one handful of louis out
of my winnings. He never had the pluck to put a
louis on the table because, as I have said, he always
felt that a gold piece was a good deal of money. In
any case, does it stand to reason that a man who
had no money wherewith to pay his solicitor's fees
was the kind of man one would take to Monte Carlo
to pay one's hotel expenses and Casino losses? No
one but a fool would pretend to believe such a
farrago of rubbish.

Wilde's friends, including the never-to-be-forgotten Robert Sherard, with the "face like a Roman
Emperor," whom Wilde thought "perfectly wonderful," have echoed the cry that I was the author of
his disaster and downfall. Even Mrs. Wilde writes
to tell Sherard that I had "marred a fine life." Mr.
Ransome, who tells his readers that he derives his

biographical facts from Ross, says it in print. All
these people should surely have been aware that the
person who ruined Oscar Wilde and brought about
his disaster and marred his life was Oscar Wilde
himself. He was not charged at the Old Bailey
for having taken proceedings against the Marquis
of Queensberry, but for having made a low, squalid
and abominable brute of himself. They prefer to
assume that he was convicted on false evidence
and to speak always of me as the author of his
débâcle. Their great point seems to be that if he
had not known me he would probably never have
been found out and might have passed down to
posterity for one of those highly respectable persons of whom he professes to be so contemptuous;
and if this be their point, I will cheerfully concede
it to them.

It was also a charge against me—again on
Wilde's word only—that I was, at the time of his
trouble, attacking him with loathsome letters. Now,
what does this mean, and what is the suggestion?
Where are those letters, and how could I be ac-
cusing him in letters on the one hand, and putting
up money to defend him from these very accusations on the other? I had written him no loathsome
letters: all I had written after our conversation on
the subject was a letter in which I confirmed my

opinion that, as he was innocent of these charges, he had no alternative but to proceed against my father. Yet this was brought against me as being as "loathsome" as the cards on which my father had been charging him with a terrible offence. The truth was that Wilde, having once decided to take proceedings against my father, made up his mind that, if they failed, I was to be responsible for everything.

CHAPTER VII

THE WILDE TRIALS

ALL the world knows that the proceedings against my father broke down, as it was only natural that they should. Wilde had a guilty mind, which he was careful to hide from me, and he attributed his defeat to "a foul and hideous conspiracy" and not to the fact that my father had merely spoken the truth. One of his biographers has given a highly melodramatic account of what happened after the collapse of the prosecution. Says the writer in question: "At that moment, my friend, with some companions, was sitting in a private room in the Cadogan Arms (*sic*), smoking cigarettes, drinking whisky-and-soda, and waiting. What for waiting (*sic*), not one of them could have said. They had set fire to a mine and were trying to stupefy themselves into the belief and hope that it would not explode beneath them. It was reported to me that when, after an intentional delay of many hours, unable to wait any longer, the police at last moved and a knock came at the door of that sitting-room in the Cadogan Arms, they all blanched as if under the shock of a sudden surprise. Not one of his friends had the sense to explain to Wilde what was the true meaning of the warning his counsel had given at the close of his cross-examination, or to force him to realise that, if only as a matter of public policy, he should leave the country at once. As a matter of fact, the warrant for his arrest was not signed until after the last day train for Dover, carefully watched, had been seen to leave without him, and it was impossible to delay action any longer."

The inexactitudes herein set forward are as beautiful as they are numerous. In the first place, this wonderful biographer's friend never sat with some companions in a private room in the Cadogan Arms smoking cigarettes and drinking whiskies and soda. Wilde's companions, for reasons best known to themselves, disappeared like snowflakes on a river the moment it was known that Sir Edward Clarke had withdrawn from the proceedings against my father. The only person left with him at this precise juncture happens to have been myself. We were both well aware that Wilde's arrest might follow on what had happened; and Wilde was not only sure that he was about to be arrested, but he told me that in all likelihood they would arrest me also.

I did my best to cheer him up, and I pointed out to
him that they were welcome to indulge in any
amount of arresting, since he said himself that he
had done nothing and I knew that I had done nothing. I had a suite of rooms at the Cadogan Hotel—
not "Arms," Mr. Sherard, if you please!—in Sloane
Street, and I drove Wilde there from the Old Bailey
after we had lunched at the Holborn Hotel. I
never saw a man more broken up or more nervously
anxious about himself. He kept on tearfully protesting that it was a vile and hideous conspiracy
against him, and that the suspense would kill him.
I managed to bring him to reason, somewhat, by
talking to him pretty plainly; and, in order to help
him with the suspense difficulty, I went down to the
House of Commons to see my cousin, George
Wyndham, and asked him if he could find out what
the authorities intended to do. Wyndham saw me
in the lobby and, after making enquiries in the
House, came out and told me that Sir Robert Reid
had told him that there was to be a prosecution. I
went back to the Cadogan Hotel and found there,
not Oscar Wilde, but a letter in which he told me
he had been arrested and would have to pass
the night at Bow Street, and asking me to see various people on the question of bail, and also to come
to Bow Street and try to see him. This letter I

had intended to produce in facsimile, but the amiable
Mr. Ross has obtained an injunction which prevents
me from doing so. There was never any question
of his leaving the country until the time when he
was out on bail. According to his own showing, he
had no reason for leaving the country other than
to avoid the inconvenience of a criminal trial. In
any case, he could not have left, because he was
shadowed by detectives from the moment he had left
the Old Bailey that morning. So far from sitting
in private rooms and endeavouring to stupefy ourselves with cigarettes and whisky, we had spent the
hour after lunch in going round to George Lewis,
the solicitor, to see if he could do anything. He
said it was too late for anything to be done, and
that if the matter had been taken to him in the first
instance, he would simply have destroyed my
father's card and told Wilde not to be a fool. In
view of Mr. Ross's attempt to attribute Wilde's
downfall to my bad advice, it is singular that I had
recommended him to go to Mr. Lewis. If he had
done so, there would have been no prosecution. As
it was, he went to Mr. Ross's own solicitor, Mr.
Humphreys, who advised the prosecution which
proved so disastrous.

I do not think that the grounds upon which Sir
Edward Clarke withdrew from the proceedings

against my father have ever been stated, and consequently I set them out herewith. Sir Edward Clarke, like myself, believed in Wilde's innocence. He looked upon him as more or less of a madman, who did everything that was foolish and unwise for the mere sake of appearing eccentric or superior; but he nevertheless believed that he was innocent of any actual viciousness. After Sir Edward Carson's cross-examination of Wilde, there was a conference, and Sir Edward Clarke pointed out that it would be impossible to get over the prejudice created in the minds of the jury by Wilde's admissions in the witness-box. Sir Edward Carson had made great use of "The Picture of Dorian Gray" in the course of the cross-examination, and passages had been read which obviously pointed to a most objectionable attitude of mind on the part of the author towards certain vices. Sir Edward Clarke advised that when the proceedings opened next day, no further evidence should be offered against the Marquis of Queensberry, and that the case against him should be abandoned on the ground that what Wilde had written and published in "Dorian Gray" would be sufficient to justify a reasonable person in supposing that Wilde sympathised with the vices in question. It should be pointed out that my father had not accused Wilde

of the actual practice of these vices; on the card
which he left at Wilde's club he had written an
accusation against Wilde as "posing" as a vicious
person. Sir Edward Clarke was of opinion that,
if the course indicated were taken, the defence
would be more or less appeased and that Wilde
would, to some extent, save his face and lessen the
risks of a subsequent prosecution. "If you withdraw from the case now," said Sir Edward, "it will
be a nine days' talk, but you will probably hear no
more about it so far as the authorities are concerned. If you continue, and Lord Queensberry is
found 'not guilty,' they will, in all probability, arrest
you in court." Mr.—now Sir Charles—Matthews,
who was also counsel for Wilde, agreed with Sir
Edward, and it was decided to withdraw. Everybody who writes about this part of the proceedings
contrives to suggest that Sir Edward Clarke threw
up the sponge in disgust and without Wilde's consent or knowledge. In point of fact, Wilde consented to the withdrawal and, so far from throwing
him over as a client, both Sir Edward Clarke and
Sir Charles Matthews defended him in the two subsequent trials, and, what is more, defended him
for nothing.

On returning to the Cadogan Hotel and finding
that Wilde had been arrested, I went straight to

Bow Street and offered bail for his temporary
release. I was told that bail could not be accepted
that night and that, if bail were accepted at all,
other securities besides myself would be required.
I went off at once to see Mr.—now Sir George—
Alexander and Mr. Lewis Waller, at whose theatres
Wilde's plays were running, and asked them to offer
bail. In the letter Wilde left for me at the Cadogan
he requested me to see these gentlemen for that
purpose. They both refused. Between the time
of his arrest and of his trial at the Old Bailey, Wilde
was kept at Holloway Prison, and either there or at
Bow Street I visited him daily for a period of three
or four weeks. There was nobody else to come
near him. His companions had left the country,
his wife would have nothing to do with him, and
his general acquaintance was going about London
protesting that it had never known him. It is the
fashion to say that I deserted him. At the Ransome trial Mr. Campbell, k.c., had the face to put
it to me that I fled the country. If a daily pilgrim-
age to Holloway and daily interviews with a pris-
oner are desertion and fleeing the country, then
my gentle detractors are right. Without the slightest intention of benefit to me, a certain person has
made public a letter which states that my daily visits
were the only things which quickened Wilde into

life. And here is a portion of a letter which I myself had occasion to write to this same person: "I saw Oscar yesterday in a private room at the police court, and he gave me your three letters and asked me to write and tell you how deeply touched he was by your kindness and sympathy and loyalty to him in his terrible and undeserved trouble. He himself is so ill and unhappy that he has not sufficient strength and energy to write, and all his time has to be devoted to preparing his defence against a diabolical conspiracy, which seems almost unlimited in its size and strength. I will not add to your sorrow by telling you of the privations and sufferings he has to endure. I have seen him three times since his arrest: once through a horrible kind of barred cage, separated from him by a space of one yard and in almost complete darkness, with twenty other people talking at the same time. This is the ordinary way, and one visit a day of a quarter of an hour is all he is allowed. After that, I managed to get an order from the Home Secretary to see him in a private room for three-quarters of an hour. And yesterday I contrived to have a fairly long interview with him at the police court. In spite of all the brutal and cowardly clamour of our disgusting newspapers, I think the sympathy of all decent men is with him, and that he will ultimately triumph; but

he has much to go through first. I have determined
to remain here and do what I possibly can, though
I am warned on all hands that my own risk is not
inconsiderable and my family implore me to go
away." It is plain, on the whole, therefore, that
desertion and fleeing the country are rather out of
the picture.

During the time that Wilde lay in Holloway
Prison I began to have a certain amount of doubt
as to his innocence. In our repeated conversations
he clung to the conspiracy fiction with considerable
persistence. As the time for the trial drew near,
however, he began to weaken, and eventually he
admitted that there were "things in his life which
could be made to look pretty awkward;" but this
was as far as he would go. His one anxiety seemed
to be that I should not give him up, and I always
told him that I never would. One day he said to
me: "Even if these horrible tales were true, you
would stick to me, wouldn't you?" And I said, "Of
course I would." It was not until the day before
the trial that he made anything like a proper attempt
to unburden himself. It had been arranged that I
should see him in a private room on this day and
that we should have a longer interview than was
permitted by the regulations. We talked on general matters for some time, but ultimately Wilde

became very serious and said that he did not see how it was possible for him to hope for a verdict of "not guilty." He then went on to tell me that, "in a way," the charges set forward in the indictment were true and that he must have been mad to live as he had been living and that his only hope was that the skill of Clarke and Matthews might save him from the severest punishment. He reminded me of my promise not to forsake him and, though I was shocked at what he told me, I am free to confess that it never entered into my head that it was my duty forthwith to give up his acquaintance. I told him that what he had said should not make any difference and that I would stick to him through thick and thin.

In the meanwhile great pressure was being brought to bear on me by my family to leave the country. My father's advisers put up the very worst reason they could have chosen to get me to do this. They pretended that, as my name had been so continually linked with Wilde's, and as a silly letter he had addressed to me had been read in court, I was under some danger of being arrested and charged with him. Such threats did not move me in the least—rather, they confirmed me in my determination to stop where I was. During those unpleasant days I seemed almost to live at Bow

Street or Holloway, so that if the police had wanted me they knew where to find me. Then Sir Edward Clarke took a hand, quite independently, I believe, of any suggestion from my family. He pointed out that my continued association with Wilde after the collapse of the case against my father was creating all sorts of comment and prejudice, and that it would be much better for Wilde if I went abroad. When I put it to Wilde he said that he quite agreed with Sir Edward Clarke and that I should be obliging him and putting him in a better position in the eyes of the world if I remained away during the trial. Even with this assurance I was not satisfied, and I asked Wilde to think it over and put it into writing, which he did. I thereupon left England for Paris. The result of the trial was that the jury disagreed. There had been six counts in the indictment, and the prosecution had brought up all sorts of extraordinary evidence, but the jury could not come to a unanimous verdict. It had been said, and, I believe, with truth, that only one juror stood out in Wilde's favour. In any case, there was the fact of no verdict, and the authorities had to consider their position. They decided to have a new trial, and Wilde was taken back to Holloway. It was arranged that he should be admitted to bail until the new trial took place if sureties to the amount of two thousand five hundred pounds were forthcoming. My brother Percy, then Lord Douglas of Hawick and now Marquis of Queensberry, and the Rev. Stuart Headlam became bail for the amount.

I have often thought that the supremely tragical period of Wilde's life was not the moment of his taking action against my father, as he suggested, but the period during which he was out on bail with the second trial looming ahead of him. I have reason for knowing that Wilde looked upon the disagreement of the jury as a sort of verdict in his favour, and was under the impression that he stood a very good sporting chance of being found not guilty at the second trial. It is notorious that persons afflicted with Wilde's particular type of viciousness are for ever believing that the world will one day condone and even approve of them. Wilde looked upon the one juryman who refused to find him guilty not as an honest Englishman who was determined to satisfy himself on the evidence, but as a friend or approver of unnameable wickedness. He argued: "If there was one man of this jury who was with me there is sure to be one on the next," and, as it was evident that people were becoming tired of the scandal, and the press, which in the beginning had pursued him with relentless

and bloodthirsty fierceness, had calmed down a
good deal, he began to think that he would get off.
For my own part, I do not profess to have had
great wisdom, but it happens that I did not think
that he would get off and, rightly or wrongly, I
advised him to leave the country. I wrote to my
brother Percy and asked him if he would mind if
Wilde made a bolt of it. The matter was put to
Wilde and he refused to budge. His brother is
reputed to have said: "Oscar is an Irish gentleman
and will face the music." It has been held up to
him for nobility that he did remain, and I have
frequently seen it stated that he remained because
he did not wish to be dishonourable with respect
to his bail. His bail, however, would not have complained if he had gone. Yet he stopped. Here
again the tragedy was entirely of his own making.
Even if we are to believe that Wilde abandoned
his will-power entirely to me when he went to Bow
Street for his warrant, how comes it to pass that
when he was at Oakley Street without a shilling or
a friend and a public exposure behind him of the
like no man ever had in all history, his will-power
suddenly reasserts itself? I have been blamed for
suggesting that he should go away. On the other
hand, the very people who blamed me for advising
his retreat when I knew that he was guilty, have

blamed me for not advising him to get away when I supposed him to be innocent. I take no shame whatever for having advised him as I did. His withdrawal to France would have cost my brother two thousand five hundred pounds, and heaven alone knows what it would have cost me in hard money; but it would have saved Wilde two years of imprisonment and it would have saved literature from the ultimate degradation at his hands. For it is obvious that, if he had remained a free man, he would not have degraded himself and the English language by writing "De Profundis."

I have already produced the statement of one of Wilde's biographers as to the manner in which Wilde and his companions are alleged to have spent the hours between the collapse of the case against Lord Queensberry and Wilde's arrest; but I should like once more to call attention to the sentence about the police knocking at the door of the sitting-room at the Cadogan Arms and the "blanched faces" and "sudden surprise" of Wilde and his companions. Here is another account of what happened: "Oscar Wilde had spent that afternoon in a private sitting-room at a hotel, smoking cigarettes, drinking whisky and soda and reading now the Yellow Book and now evening papers. *He evinced neither dismay nor trepidation when the officers entered the room,* and, on alighting from the cab at Scotland Yard, he had a courteous discussion with one of the detectives about the payment of the cab." It will interest the reader to know that both these accounts, though they are diametrically opposed one to the other, are the work of the same person—namely, Robert Harborough Sherard.

It is the same Mr. Sherard who tells the following fearful and wonderful anecdote: "Late in the afternoon of the following day, Saturday, 25th May, 1895, Oscar Wilde was found guilty and sentenced to two years' hard labour. There had been six counts against him. He was asked after his release by a very old friend as to the justice of the finding, and he said: 'Five of the counts referred to matters with which I had absolutely nothing to do. There was some foundation for one of the counts.' 'But then, why,' asked his friend, 'did you not instruct your defenders?' 'That would have meant betraying a friend,' said Oscar. Circumstances which have since transpired have established—what for the rest was never in doubt in the minds of those who heard it made—the absolute truth of this statement."

Presuming that Wilde said this, he must have taken for granted that "those who heard him" had suddenly become idiots. The six counts of the in-

DRAWING OF LORD ALFRED DOUGLAS, AT THE
AGE OF TWENTY-FOUR

dictment bore reference to his improper relations with different persons, all of whom were produced in the witness-box and gave their evidence in Wilde's presence. If a friend had been involved in the slightest way, that friend's name would most assuredly have leaked out in the course of the proceedings, and if twenty friends had been involved and their names had been kept secret, Wilde's position would not have been bettered in the slightest degree or his guilt any the less plainly established. Wilde was not of the stuff that goes to hard labour with the name of a friend in his bosom when, by mentioning that name, he could have cleared himself. His whole principle of life was subversive to any such high altruism; he would not have gone without his dinner to save a friend—much less have faced ruin and imprisonment.

CHAPTER VIII

HARD LABOUR AND AFTER

TO say that I was distressed by the sentence of two years' imprisonment with hard labour, imposed upon Wilde by a Judge who seemed to be absolutely without mercy, is to put a mild term upon my condition of anguish. Wilde and his supporters never ceased to suggest that the whole thing was my fault. They never blamed him for what he had done, but went about calling my father opprobrious names and asserting that I had been Wilde's ruin. It pleased them to have a scapegoat upon whom to shift the moral responsibilities of this big fat man and, with the help of a foolish letter or two which I had written at moments of great stress, they shifted them to some purpose. I have no desire to be mealy-mouthed about the suggestions which have been made, and I will say right out what impression it is that these people have tried to create from the time that Wilde went to prison. They have suggested that I, Alfred Bruce Douglas, was a partner in the vices of which Wilde was charged and convicted. There has been more or less established the legend that it was I who took him from the path of rectitude and introduced him to the kennels of foulness; and the impression has been created that I led a debauched life with him prior to his imprisonment and that, when he came out and was willing to mend his ways and be reconciled to his wife, it was I who seduced him and dragged him back to his old villainies. I observe that Mr. Ransome has the following note to the edition of his critical study which has lately been published at a shilling: "The publication of this book in 1912 was the subject of a libel action which was brought against me in the King's Bench Division of the High Court of Justice, and was heard before Mr. Justice Darling and a Special Jury on four days in April, 1913. In that action a verdict was given in my favour. In bringing out this new edition I have considered the question of reprinting the book in its original form, as I have a perfect right to do; but as I do not consider that the passages complained of are essential to the critical purpose of my book, I have decided, in order to spare the feelings of those who might be pained by the further publication of those passages, to omit them from this edition."

Mr. Ransome's desire to spare people's feelings by omitting from his book what is not true is wonderfully creditable to him; but the fact remains that he asserted in his first edition that Wilde owed some, at least, of the circumstances of his public disgrace to me, while the exquisite Mr. Sherard goes further and embellishes his "authoritative" life with the following passage: "He was then living in Naples. The circumstances under which he had been obliged to leave Berneval and return to *the least desirable companionship that the world of men offered to his choice* are summed up in the following sentence by the author of 'Twenty Years in Paris': 'The time came, however, when, being without money, repulsed, desolate, he could no longer resist entreaties which offered to him companionship in the place of utter loneliness, friendship in the place of hostility, homage in the place of insult and, in the place of impending destitution, a luxurious and elegant hospitality.' "

It is well known that it was I who offered him a sanctuary at Naples when his money had run out and he was reduced to a paltry allowance of two pounds nineteen and sixpence a week; and I submit that the sentence italicised in the above-quoted passage is intended to mean—and can only mean— one thing; while Ransome's assertion is capable of the worst interpretation. And now we come to the inner secret of the whole of the abominable business. When Wilde went to prison I was in France, by his own request. I wrote to him the moment I heard of the sentence, and there can be no doubt whatever that, up to this point, we were good friends and that he counted me his chiefest and dearest friend. I set to work immediately to do what I could for him in the way of trying to get his sentence reduced, and trying to obtain for him special privileges in prison. In pursuance of my promise and my natural desire to stick to him through thick and thin, I even went the length of writing to certain newspapers with a view to showing that what he had done would not have been considered so very terrible by many eminent people; that his offence was no offence at all in France, and that his sentence was altogether out of proportion to his crime when one came to consider the amount of suffering a sentence of two years' hard labour would entail upon a man of his nature and temperament.

In addition to engaging myself in these efforts on Wilde's behalf, I was kept continually busy repelling all sorts of stupid attacks on myself. Wilde's conviction and the curiosity and scandal aroused by what transpired at the trial seems to

have driven the whole of Paris into a state of madness for the time being. Statements of the most
ridiculous kind about Wilde and myself were published broadcast—articles were printed which purported to be written by me and were signed in my
name, though I had never so much as seen them;
and one paper went the length of printing a number
of gallant letters which I was alleged to have addressed to a certain well-known *demi-mondaine*—
a lady, by the way, to whom I had never written
or spoken in my life. I spent a great deal of time
and temper in endeavouring to cope with these
matters: I challenged various people to duels and I
took actions at law against various newspapers.
But I soon found that it was next door to impossible
to keep track of my traducers and that I might
easily have spent the rest of my life in litigation
without obtaining redress.

About this time I wrote for the *Mercure de
France* an article about Wilde which might have
done him a certain amount of good in the literary
sense. Sherard heard in some way that this article
had been written; he mentioned it to Wilde in prison
and, on the strength of what Wilde said, Sherard
wrote me a letter stating that Wilde desired that
the article should not appear. I gave Sherard his
immediate and proper answer and, as it was noth-

ing to me whether the article appeared or not, unless Wilde wished it to appear, I arranged with the *Mercure de France* that it should not be printed. In the meantime, I decided to go to England and to visit Wilde in prison, in order that we might talk generally of his affairs. I wrote informing Robert Ross of my intention and, in reply, he told me that he had just come from Wilde and that, as his correspondence and visitors were strictly limited, he desired that I should neither write to him nor visit him. I said that I thought such a request ought to have come to me directly from Wilde— either by word of mouth or by letter—but Ross told me that prisoners were allowed to write only a limited number of letters in the year, and to see only a limited number of visitors and that he had already written as many letters as he was entitled to write and would be unable either to receive letters or visitors for some time to come. I was very much upset on receiving this news, and I had some thought of trying to obtain an interview with Wilde through influence which I possessed; but I was told that it would be bad for Wilde if I did so, and I accordingly determined to follow out his wishes and to wait until he could write or send to me. I subsequently went to Naples and occupied myself with literary pursuits, getting together a volume of poetry which I proposed to publish and dedicate to Wilde.

Now it is quite clear that during the latter part of his imprisonment Wilde laboured under the impression that my silence and my failure to visit him were due to carelessness, indifference and apathy on my part. Either he did not know, or pretended not to know, of the precise intimations given to me not to visit or write to him. As he did not hear from me, he concluded that I had forsaken him. This filled him with a violent anger, and he set to work and wrote "De Profundis." His rage and hate apparently knew no limits, and Sherard published a letter of Mrs. Wilde's, in which she states that she had seen her husband in prison and that he had said that if he could get hold of ——, meaning myself, he would kill him.

And all this time I was thinking hourly of the man who had been my friend and counting the days to the time of his release. I had steady reports of him from Ross, but never a word or a hint that he was angry with me or that I had done anything to offend him, until he had nearly completed his sentence. The only indication of the sort that came my way was in the matter of the dedication of my first volume of poems. Ross wrote to say that Wilde felt that it would be better if I did not dedicate the book to him; and, as he wished it, I refrained and issued the book without any dedication at all.

Of Wilde in prison we have had many touching and woeful pictures. Sherard has a passage about it which, in the circumstances, is worth quoting: "In Wandsworth Prison first and then in Reading Gaol, Oscar Wilde's mental development reached a point of transcendency to which never in the world of men he could have hoped to attain. There had been forced upon him the recluse life which had raised many men in the world's history towards the stars, but which, perhaps, never before demonstrated its reforming and enhancing powers in a manner more magnificent, more orbicular, more triumphant. In the old days he had tried to imitate Balzac in his mode of life; but Society and Pleasure had ever knocked at the door of his cell, nor had he the strength of will great enough to resist their allurements. Now there were iron bars between him and the wasteful pleasures of the world: a claustration as strict, if less severe, than that which Balzac imposed upon himself, held him fast, and he had the time to think. He had the time to think, and with a brain which at last had recovered its splendid normal power. The prison *régime,* the enforced temperance in food, the enforced abstin-

ence from all narcotic drugs and drink, the regular
hours, the periodical exercise—the simple life, in
one word—had restored him the splendid heritage
that he had received from nature. What the real
Oscar Wilde was, and of what he was capable, was
now to be made patent. In 'De Profundis' he laid
his soul bare, and the impartial are to judge from
that book of the man's new powers as a thinker
and as a literary artist. His friends will ask no
more than that, reserving to themselves the high
delight of taking a holy joy in the lofty virtues
which that book reveals, the kindness, the patience,
the resignation, the forgiveness of sins so splendid
that one may almost believe that in his ardent medi-
tations on Christ he was able to bring the bodily
presence of the God who taught these things into
his cell, and to learn from the divine lips themselves
what is the true secret of human happiness. Critics
abroad have said: 'There is too much about Christ
in "De Profundis," ' overlooking the fact that the
book is, from the first page to the last, inspired by
Christ—that no man who had not found Christ
could have written that book, nor lived as the man
who wrote it did live. In England, one heard it
said that it is absurd to believe that an agnostic, a
sensualist would turn to religion, and the blas-
phemous statement has been made that this book

is, in its way, no more sincere than the dying confessions of many prison cells, the greasy cant that officious chaplains win from fawning prisoners. One has heard the word HYPOCRISY pronounced." This is very precious writing and quite typical of the ecstatic frame of mind of the average Wilde enthusiast. Unlike Mr. Ransome, however, Mr. Sherard does not appear to have had the advantage of knowing that the published "De Profundis," which aroused him to such a pitch of pietistic fervour, is merely a collection of elegant extracts. A perusal of the extracts from the complete "De Profundis" published in reports of the Ransome trial would have convinced him that this saint-like inhabitant of Wandsworth and Reading gaols was indeed a hypocrite of the most hypocritical dye, and that the "De Profundis" was indeed "no more sincere than the dying confessions of many prison cells, the greasy cant that officious chaplains wring from fawning prisoners." Nay, it was worse than this, for the design of the canting deceiver of prison chaplains is not usually to hurt other people, whereas Wilde's design was utterly to destroy the reputation and good name of a man who had befriended him; and to do this in such a way that he might still continue to obtain kindness and money from the object of his hatred and leave him absolutely without a word of defence in his lifetime. I say that Oscar Wilde conceived this horrible and unheard-of plot in his unreasoning rage at what he conceived to be my attitude towards him, and I say that Mr. Robert Ross, who professed great friendship for me both then and until long after Wilde's death, did nothing to make Wilde's plot. ineffective, or even to warn me of it. On the contrary, he presented the unpublished parts of "De Profundis" to the authorities at the British Museum on the understanding that it was to remain sealed up only until the year 1960. However, I shall deal with the whole question of "De Profundis" in a separate chapter. My main point here is to show plainly what has been brought to my charge, and to show how the people who bring these charges stultify themselves. Nobody who reads Mr. Ransome's book before (out of the kindness of his heart) he removed his aspersions on me, could doubt for a moment that he wished to convey the impression that I had a bad influence upon Wilde and that it was this bad influence that brought Wilde to grief and prevented him from rehabilitating himself after his release. Yet it is this same Mr. Ransome—who tells his readers in his preface that he is indebted to Mr. Ross for verifications of his biographical facts—who gives us the following precise details as to "the intensification of Wilde's personality" when he became a habitual devotee of the vice for which he was imprisoned: *"He had first experimented in that vice,"* says Ransome, *"in 1886; his experiments became a habit in 1889."* Well, in 1886 I was a boy, fifteen years of age, at Winchester School, and I had never so much as heard of Oscar Wilde; whereas in 1889 I was eighteen years of age and in the south of France with a tutor, and was not to meet Wilde—whose name was still unknown to me—till nearly three years later. So that by the time we did meet he had already found his way to the lowest moral depths without my juvenile assistance. It is to be noted further that both Ross and Sherard knew Wilde long before I did; and, according to their own showing, were his constant and faithful companions until I arrived on the scene. Both of them swear that they never heard him use an objectionable phrase or an obscene remark, and that they had no inkling of his aberration. Whereas I, a callow undergraduate from Oxford, with so simple an outlook upon life that, in spite of my classical training, I never clearly understood the nature of Wilde's viciousness till the time of the trials, am alleged to have known everything and to have been the prime mover in events which had occurred years before I was on the scene at all.

Then again, let us take the accounts of what happened immediately after Wilde came out of prison. During the time of his incarceration some sympathiser or other—a lady, by the way—put up a thousand pounds for the use of Wilde, so that he might have money by him while he was in prison and a sufficient sum to face the world with when he came out. There can be no doubt whatever that Wilde had at least eight hundred pounds at his command on the day he left prison. Ransome tells us that he "immediately crossed the Channel for Dieppe, where he stayed for some days and drove about with Mr. Robert Ross and Mr. Reginald Turner, examining the surrounding villages, most of which seemed uninhabitable." At the end of a week he took rooms in the inn at the little hamlet of Berneval. Then he took a châlet for the season and talked about building a house. "He asked for his pictures and Japanese gold-paper that should provide a fitting background for lithographs by Rothenstein and Shannon." Sherard tells us that at Berneval his resources melted away in his hands. "He spent money with the recklessness of sailors on shore and prisoners free of gaol. . . . In inviting friends to visit him at Berneval, he used to ask those

who were married to bring their wives with them.
. . . He showed himself, to those who had the
privilege of seeing him during the weeks he spent in
Berneval, *a gentleman, a hero, and a Christian!*"
Doubtless! The italics are mine and I make no
comment. I was in Paris and, later, in Aix-les-
Bains with my mother during the brief, bright,
brotherly Berneval weeks, when Oscar Wilde was
getting rid of the last of his substance and throwing
out of the window, as it were, the money which
should have been used reasonably to maintain him
until he could cast about for work. I heard from
Wilde that he was all right and going well and
strong, and that he had "dear so-and-so" and "dear
so-and-so" to visit him. Several letters passed between us, and he kept on saying that he would come
to see me. Ultimately, when I had decided to take
a villa at Naples, it was arranged that Wilde should
visit me there. Just before I started for Naples, I
got a long letter, in which he explained that he had
spent his last shilling, that all his friends were gone,
and that he hadn't even sufficient money to pay his
fare to Naples. I telegraphed a sufficient sum to
cover his expenses and he joined me there at the
Royal Hotel. Soon after I moved into the Villa
Giudice at Posilippo, taking Wilde with me. In less
than three months at Berneval he had got through

eight hundred pounds, and he came to me penniless, excepting for what I had myself given him. It is suggested that his coming to Naples was the result of frantic appeals and persuasions on my part. In point of fact, he came because he had nowhere else to go and because nobody else would have him. He required neither "luring" nor "tempting"—which he certainly would not have had from me, in any case—and he was very glad to find a refuge in my establishment.

There is just one other point, and I shall have done with this very unpleasant part of my subject. The people who suggest that in some unexplained manner I was the means of separating Wilde from his wife forget that Wilde left prison in May, 1897, and did not join me at Naples until the end of August of the same year. We have seen that immediately on his release from prison he went to Dieppe and was driving about with Ross and Turner. Why did they not take him to his wife? They were with him for weeks at Berneval, and so was Sherard. Why was the reconciliation—which Sherard professes to have laboured like Hercules to arrange—never brought about? Of course, the answer is Alfred Douglas stood between them. The fact is, that Alfred Douglas did nothing of the sort. What actually happened was this: Wilde never dreamed of rejoining Mrs. Wilde or becoming reconciled to her while his money lasted.   When his money was spent he wrote to Ross and asked if more could not be raised.   Ross replied that nothing more could be done.   Wilde then wrote to his wife to enquire if she would receive him as her husband. Wilde asserted that she sent him a reply full of hums and haws and imposed a number of what he described as absurd conditions.   The letter drove him into a fury and, I believe, he never wrote again to her in his life, or she to him.   The plain fact is— as the unpublished part of "De Profundis" shows— that Wilde had never forgiven me for what he believed to be my neglect of him while he was in prison; and that if the supplies of money had held out, he would never have come near me.   But when he found that his admirers and supporters in London were not disposed to keep him in the lap of luxury at Berneval, and that they considered his miserable pittance of under three pounds a week sufficient for him to live upon, his thoughts turned towards Naples, where he knew no such views of economy were likely to prevail.   He came to me on false pretences, because he knew that "De Profundis" had not been destroyed and, from that time forward to the day of his death, I had the honour and pleasure of supporting him.

CHAPTER IX

WHEN Wilde came to the Villa Giudice he was in fair health and reasonable spirits. That he had eaten and drunk too much at Berneval he freely admitted, but on the whole he was in good physical condition. From the end of August to the middle of November he had the run of my villa as my guest, and I paid the whole of the housekeeping expenses, including the tradesmen's bills for food and wine, the servants' wages, and so forth, to which expenses Wilde never so much as contributed a farthing piece. So far as I am aware, the life he lived here was perfectly proper and without reproach. He had brought with him from Berneval a rough draft of part of the "Ballad of Reading Gaol," which he read to me. It has been stated on supposed authority that Wilde composed none of the "Ballad of Reading Gaol" during the time of his imprisonment. He told me that he had composed certain of the stanzas in prison and he added to them at

Berneval. But there can be no question that the poem was completed at Naples. He laboured over it in a manner which I had never known him to labour before. Every word had to be considered; every rhyme and every cadence carefully pondered. I had "Ballad of Reading Gaol" for breakfast, dinner and tea, and for many weeks it was almost our sole topic of conversation. For my own part, I, too, was busy with literary work, and I wrote at Naples during this period some of my best sonnets, and occupied myself with various translations. We had not an idle week during the whole time we were together. It was one of the charges against me in the Ransome case that I hindered Wilde in his literary production, and that he never did anything worth doing when he was with me. How maliciously false these statements were may be gathered from the fact that he planned and wrote the whole of "A Woman of No Importance" while we were together at Lady Mount-Temple's house at Babbacombe; that he wrote the whole of "The Importance of Being Earnest" at Worthing, where we shared a house; and "The Ideal Husband" partly at Goring, where we shared a house, and partly in London, while we were continually together; while he composed and completed the final version of the "Ballad of Reading Gaol" whilst staying in my villa at Naples. I have no desire to take credit to myself for another man's work, but many collaborations between authors have been acknowledged on much less slender grounds than it would be possible for me to set up in the matter of the aforesaid plays and of the aforesaid "Ballad of Reading Gaol" if I were disposed to do so. In the ordinary course of events I would never have said a single word on the subject. It seemed to me perfectly natural that, as we were together, Wilde should show me what he was doing and read me what he was writing. And as he thereby invited advice and criticism, it seemed to be perfectly natural that I should give it, and that he should adopt it. The truth is that Wilde consistently made free use of such gifts as I possessed, that I assisted him to many a piece of dialogue and many a gibe which has helped to make him famous, and that I gave him very material aid and counsel in the matter of the "Ballad of Reading Gaol." There are passages in this latter poem which he lifted holus-bolus from a poem of my own, and it must be remembered that, while up to the time that he left Reading Gaol, he had affected some scorn of the ballad form and knew next to nothing of its possibilities, I had given a great amount of attention to the study of that form and had produced the "Ballad of Perkin Warbeck" and the "Ballad of St. Vitus"—which latter Wilde read for the first time at Naples, and with which he was mightily impressed. It would be preposterous for me to claim more than my due as regards the literary side of our friendship, and I had perhaps better put the position this way: I have never denied that I learned things from Wilde and that, up to a certain point, I owe a good deal to him in the literary sense. On the other hand, in view of what he said, it is necessary for me to point out that Wilde owes just as much to me as I owe to him and, for that matter, a great deal more. I have written neither plays nor poems which embody a single word or phrase of his, and I never took a literary hint from him in my life. He has done me the honour to use a great deal of Alfred Douglas, and he is perfectly welcome. All I ask is, that I may not be maligned in consequence.

Although our life at the Villa Giudice was perfectly harmless and consisted mainly of fairly strenuous literary toil, the fact that we were together did not please certain of Wilde's friends, and the scandal-mongers were set busy again. How easy it is to make scandal was prettily illustrated by no less a personage than Mr. Justice Darling during the course of the Ransome trial. "Are you aware, Mr. Campbell," said his lordship to the defending counsel, "are you aware of the reputation of Naples?" Of course, Mr. Campbell shook his head in the most deprecatory manner, and the jury made a mental note that a villa at Naples meant the very lowest depths of wickedness and profligacy.

Anybody who knows Europe at all, knows perfectly well that Naples was then, and is now, a resort of the most exclusive set of the Italian aristocracy, and that there is a large and highly respectable English colony there. My grandmother, the late Hon. Mrs. Alfred Montgomery, lived there for twenty years, and there was not a person of position in the place by whom I was not known or with whom I was not on calling terms if I cared to follow up my social duties. There is nothing at all about the reputation of Naples to differentiate it from Rome or Genoa or Florence or Venice or any other Italian city. Many people of distinction whom Mr. Justice Darling might not be sorry to know continue to make a point of going there every season. Well, just as there were brave men before Agamemnon, so there were people who could ferret out scandal even from the most harmless method of life before Mr. Justice Darling. Wilde and I were together at Naples, and malice and leering gossip were abroad with their abominable insinuations before one had time to say "jackknife." The

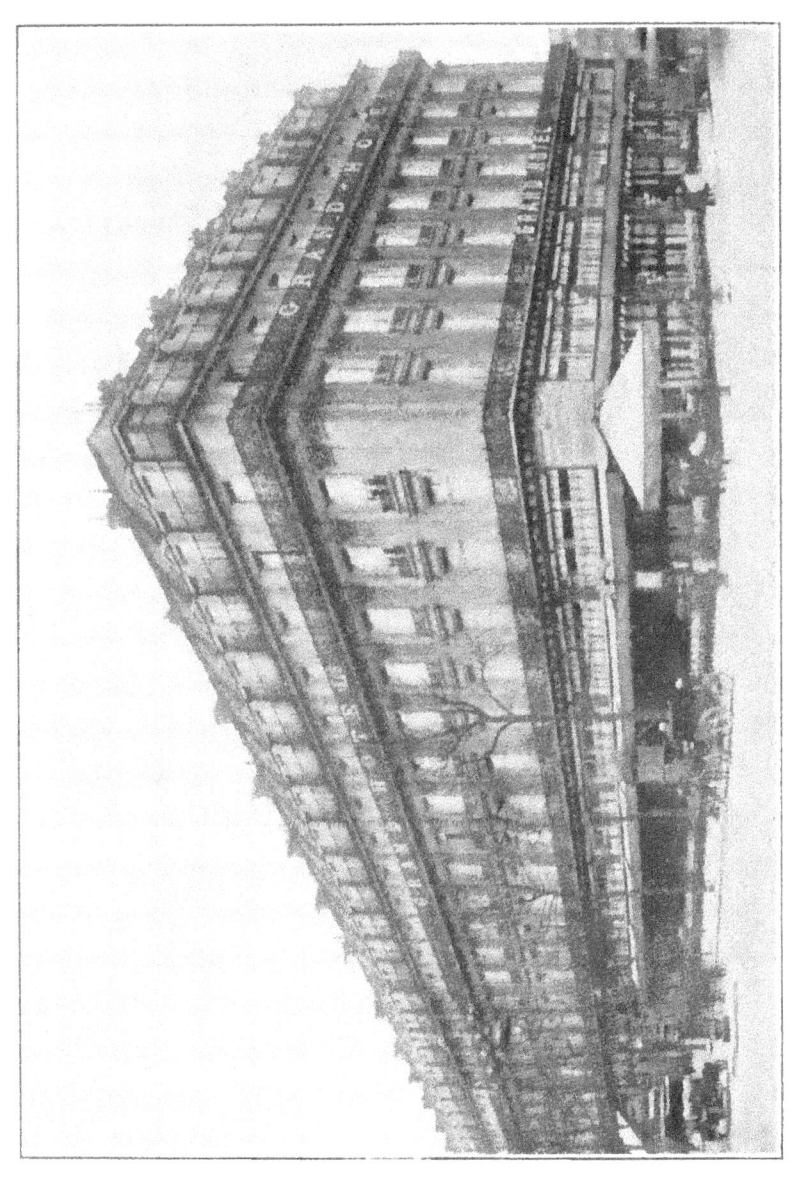

CAFÉ DE LA PAIX, PARIS

reports naturally came to the ears of my people,
who were much distressed and upset by them; and
it was pointed out to me that I was doing myself
great damage by befriending this man and that I
ought to send him about his business. One of the
attachés from the British Embassy at Rome, in
which city I had spent the winter of 1896 with my
mother, came to Naples, at the instigation of the
Ambassador, expressly to see me, and to urge on
me the advisability of dissociating myself from
Wilde. He told me that the fact that I had Wilde
as a guest in my house was causing all sorts of unpleasant gossip, and he even went so far as to say
that it was not fair to them at the Embassy that I
should persist in giving cause for such gossip, as
they had all made a point of being civil and friendly
to me when I was in Rome. I told him that I cared
nothing for gossip and scandal, that I had asked
Wilde to stay with me because he had nowhere else
to go and was practically without means, and that
it was unthinkable that in these circumstances I
should turn him out of my house simply because
evil-minded people chose to concern themselves
with what was no affair of theirs. He was very
insistent, and when he found that I was not to be
moved he got annoyed with me, told me I was a
"quixotic fool" and that I should live to be very

sorry for having befriended a "beast like Wilde," who would get everything he could out of me and then probably turn round and abuse me. I was very indignant at this prophetic pronouncement, and we parted in anger. I believed then—and I believe now—that my attitude was the right one, and the gentlemanly one, in the right sense of the word. I knew that Oscar Wilde was hard at work on his poem. I believed that his life was clean and that he had determined to keep from his old evil courses; and I knew that my life was just as proper as it always had been, and I consequently saw no reason for turning upon my friend. The world was welcome to shrug its shoulders if it cared to, and I proposed to leave it to its shrugging. But the feeling amongst my friends in England, largely got up and fomented by my enemies, ultimately became so strong that it was proposed to stop my financial supplies unless I consented to a separation from Wilde. I was thus forced to capitulate; but I did not do so without a struggle and without making provision for the man who was dependent upon me. I arranged to leave him at the Villa Giudice, the rent of which had been paid in advance, and I arranged that my mother should send him two hundred pounds, which would enable him to live in comfort for a month or two; and I further arranged to let him have additional money as he wanted it. I make special reference to the sum of two hundred pounds because it is a payment which can be authenticated, and, in fact, was authenticated at the Ransome trial. It is true that at the very moment when he was writing to me in acknowledgment of these sums and to express his gratitude for my kindness, he was complaining to Ross in a letter produced at the Ransome trial that I had deserted him because his money was done. But every one with the slightest knowledge of Wilde's affairs knows perfectly well that all the money Wilde had was the allowance of two pounds nineteen and odd which came to him weekly through his friends.

The general untrustworthiness of Wilde's accusation is obvious on the face of it. Any one acquainted with him would, moreover, have laughed at his impudence in saying that I expected him to raise money. I knew Wilde too well to expect him to raise money, even in his alleged palmy days; and that I should have been ass enough to suppose that when he came to me at Naples, an ex-convict, an undischarged bankrupt, and on a railway ticket that I had paid for, he could be financially useful to me is too ridiculous for words. Yet Ransome gets into "the Critical Study" the following choice

sentences: "Soon after Wilde left Berneval for
Naples, those who controlled the allowance that
enabled him to live with his friend, purposely
stopped it. His friend, as soon as there was no
money, left him. 'It was,' said Wilde, 'a most bitter
experience in a bitter life.' He went to Paris." The
last sentence should have had an addendum: it
should have read: "He went to Paris with two hundred pounds of Lord Alfred Douglas's money in his
pocket, which had been sent to him per Mr. More
Adey and the Marchioness of Queensberry." But
it doesn't. Of course Wilde went to Paris—and he
went the moment he heard I was proposing to live
there. It was in December of 1897 that he came
and took an apartment at a hotel in the Rue Mar-
sollier. A few weeks later I came to Paris and
became the tenant of a flat in the Avenue Kléber.
He might just as well have lived at my flat for the
use he made of his hotel except to sleep in. For a
whole year—that is to say, down to the end of 1898
—he used my flat as though it were his own, invariably turning up at meal-times when he had
nowhere else to lunch or dine, and never failing
to extract from me a good deal more than I could,
at that period, afford to give him in the way of
money to tide him over his constant and ever-
recurring "difficulties." I believe that from time

to time he picked up various sums of money on his own. In January or February of 1898 he published the "Ballad of Reading Gaol" through Leonard Smithers; and later I believe he obtained some small advances of money from theatrical managers for plays which he was always going to write but of which he never produced a line. The rights of one of these he seems to have sold for sums varying from twenty to a hundred pounds to at least half a dozen different persons; and he also sold for small sums the plots of two plays and several short stories which have since been given to the public by another hand. But whatever money he got did him no good. A couple of hundred francs would take him away from his dinner at the Avenue Kléber to do himself well with a roaring company of *boulevardiers;* but the next day he was back at lunch, full of complaints of the hardness of the world and full of groans over his difficulties. I speedily came to consider him in the light of a permanent pensioner, and my servants had instructions to give him food, and not infrequently lent him money in my absence.

During 1899 and 1900 his condition went from bad to worse. At the end of 1899 I took a shooting-box in Scotland, jointly with my brother Douglas of Hawick, and I was in Scotland until the death of my father in January, 1900. I came into a considerable amount of money under my father's will, and the very first payment I made out of my inheritance was one hundred pounds, which I sent to Oscar Wilde in Paris. Out of this money he took a trip to Switzerland. By the time he came back I was at the Hotel Condé in Chantilly, where I had acquired a racing stable. Of course, I was often in Paris, and whenever I was there I made a point of asking Wilde to lunch or dine, and I never left him without handing him sums of money. My pass-books show that in a single year after the death of my father I gave Wilde nearly four hundred pounds in cheques alone: the figures appear in my bank-book and were proved at the Ransome trial: and I must have given him twice as much in hard cash or notes. At the very least penny, he had from me that year quite a thousand pounds over and above more or less constant entertainment. It was almost impossible for me to take a meal with him and keep money in my pocket. He would come to the restaurant or hotel where we were to meet with a dejected and depressed look on him, as who should say: "Behold, how we are harassed and reduced, and in what pain of mind we exist." I would give him of the best to cheer and comfort him, but his spirits insisted on remaining damp, and it was only

GRAND CAFÉ, PARIS

with difficulty that one could get a smile out of him.
When the time came for parting; if I put my hand
in my pocket and handed him five or six hundred
francs, well and good; if not, he would order another old brandy and open up a dreadful tale as to
the condition of his bill at the hotel, the attitude
of his landlord about it, and his own desperation
and despair. In the end I got more or less into the
habit of handing him what I proposed to give him
before we proceeded to refresh ourselves. I found
that by this means the old Oscar Wilde was brought
to the front, and we could talk pleasantly together,
as gentlemen should.

I remember a certain occasion on which one of
our sittings had been prolonged until a very late
hour. I had taken the precaution to hand him a
note for a thousand francs before we sat down to
dine. He took his usual abundant share of the good
things, and we talked and laughed over our string
of liqueurs and let dull care go his own way. When
I called for the bill, Wilde suddenly pulled a long
and piteous face. "My dear boy," he said, "money
—ah!—money. I hate to distress you, but I really
must have a thousand francs now. I cannot return
to my hotel unless I have with me money to pay at
least a part of the bill. I don't mind telling you
that I am without a penny in the world, and if I

do not go to the hotel to-night I shall be homeless."

"But, my dear Oscar," I said, "I have just given you a thousand francs, which you put in your pocket." He looked at me as one amazed and then burst into a fit of coughing laughter. I laughed too.

Though he could have lived quite comfortably on what I gave him, and though he had, as we have seen, a weekly allowance which should at least have kept him from starvation, there can be no doubt that towards the end of his life Wilde underwent a certain amount of privation. He resorted to all sorts of desperate shifts to get money, and composed many very plausible begging letters; but, just as pretty well every decent door was shut to him, so people had begun to steel their hearts against him, especially as he was now drinking in a most reckless way and made no secret of the fact that he had once more given himself over to his old habits. He became a sort of show for the bohemians of Paris; the sport and mock of the Boulevard and the reproach of English letters in the City of Light. He got his dinners on credit, and borrowed money from waiters. His health was on the down grade in consequence of the intensification by alcohol of a terrible disease he had contracted. He took to weeping and cursing at the slightest provocation, and, though his wit would flame out and his learning remained with him to the last, it was a poor wreck and shadow of himself which I saw from time to time when I went to Paris on various occasions in the year 1900. All through my acquaintance with him after his release from prison it had required a good deal of pluck to be seen about with him. He was known and notorious wherever we went, and I have seen men leave *cafés* because he had entered, and heard lulls in conversation and unpleasant gibes when we have visited restaurants together. At some of the places which we frequented they would have turned him out had it not been for the fact that apparently they could not afford to turn me out. In his later period the feeling against him grew more and more pronounced. His companionships and resorts were of the vilest and his self-respect was almost entirely gone.

Of Wilde's life in Paris before he began to break up, the following is a good sample daily itinerary: He would rise late, say at half-past eleven or twelve o'clock, and walk from his hotel in the Latin Quarter, through the Louvre to the *Café de la Paix,* where he would sit and drink *apéritifs* before going to lunch. In the afternoon he would go on to the *Grand Café,* where he would drink till dinner-time. The evening he generally spent where his friends might lead him, and some of them led him to pretty dreadful places. When I came to Paris from Chantilly, if I had not made an appointment with him beforehand I could always find him at the *Grand Café* or the *Café de la Paix* of a morning, or at the *Café Julien* or the *Calisaya Bar* of an afternoon. So long as I remained in Paris he lunched and dined with me as a matter of course—*Paillard's, Maire's,* and the *Café de la Paix* being our chief resorts. At his meals he behaved always like a pleased child, provided, that is to say, you had put him into a decent humour with a present of money beforehand. He was the biggest eater I ever knew, and the only man I ever met in my life who could drink quantities of champagne at each meal and keep on doing it. He had a fine head for drink, and it was not until eighteen months or so before his death that he began to lose it. Intoxication would come over him suddenly and without apparent warning. He would rise from his seat and say: "My dear fellow, I am sorry, but I perceive that I am drunk." Then he would call loudly for a cab and stumble forth. He made a great joke about these drunken fits, and one day said to me: "I have made a wonderful discovery: I find that alcohol taken persistently and in sufficiently large quantities produces all the effects of intoxication," and so it certainly did. At *Maire's* there was a real 1800 brandy, which had originally been laid down at the Tuileries. Wilde had some of it after a dinner there, and immediately began to make *Maire's* his home. The stuff cost five or six francs a glass, but this was nothing to Wilde if he happened to have money or was the guest of somebody else. He used to compliment the *maître d'hôtel* on this "excellent brandy," and there was no getting him away from it. Wilde had few friends other than myself who could be of use to him financially. Frank Harris used to come over occasionally and take him to dine at *Durand's,* and I know that Harris also obliged him with money. From time to time, too, he picked up odd acquaintances who had means and were disposed to show him kindness; but for the most part they were Americans, and their capacity for befriending the man whom one of them described as "England's premier poet-dramatist" exhibited a great want of staying power.

I was in Scotland shooting when I had a letter from Ross to say that Wilde was ill but that it was nothing serious. On the next day I got a telegram announcing that he was dead and asking what should be done in regard to his affairs. I went straight to Paris and to the Hotel d'Alsace, where Wilde lay dead. I there saw Ross and Turner. They told me that Wilde had no money. I promptly provided funds for the expenses of the moment and I paid for the funeral, at which Ross, Turner and myself were the only English mourners. After the funeral Ross handed me a list of small debts of Wilde's, consisting of unpaid dinner-bills and sums he had borrowed from waiters and such-like, the amount being between twenty and thirty pounds. These obligations I paid.

When Wilde had been dead three years I received from a M. Du Bouché, dentist of Paris, a letter in which he pointed out that Wilde had owed him six hundred francs for professional services, and that the account had never been paid. I wrote to M. Du Bouché, advising him to apply to Mr. Adrian Hope, who, I understood, was Wilde's trustee. Later Du Bouché wrote to tell me that he had applied to Mr. Adrian Hope, but that Mr. Hope professed to know nothing of Wilde's affairs or to be in any way responsible. In the face of this letter I paid M. Du Bouché six hundred francs in settlement of the account and got his receipt for it. There was no question at that time of Ross being Wilde's legal representative. Wilde made no will, but over and over again before he died he said to me: "Of course, if I die first, you will look after my literary affairs." Ross was made literary executor of Wilde's estate in 1906—six years after Wilde's

HÔTEL D'ALSACE, PARIS

death.   After the funeral he came to me and said:
"Wilde has left nothing but a tumble of old papers.
I suppose you don't mind if I go through them?"
I told him to do what he thought best, and there the
matter ended.   Ross was a person whom Wilde and
I found useful because he was always willing to
attend to occasional matters of business for us
which we were too indolent to attend to ourselves,
and this was the light in which I regarded him when
I acquiesced in the suggestion which he then made.
One would think from the continual references to
Wilde's allowance being paid to him "through Mr.
Ross" that Wilde was in some way in a condition
of tutelage to Ross.   As a matter of fact, Wilde
arranged for the payment through Ross simply to
save himself the trouble and annoyance of corre-
sponding with his wife's solicitors.

CHAPTER X

THE "BALLAD OF READING GAOL"

IF Wilde is to last as a poet it will be on the strength of the "Ballad of Reading Gaol." The "Sphinx" may also endure, though its chances—for reasons which I shall explain in the chapter on Wilde's poetry, are not comparable with those of the "Ballad." Criticism of the work itself is not entirely my present purpose. It is a work which stands out head and shoulders above any other of Wilde's performances by virtue of its human appeal and its relative freedom from defects which render the bulk of Wilde's poetry practically unreadable. It is singular, too, as being the only work of importance which Wilde completed after his imprisonment. There is a story, and I believe a true one, to the effect that before Wilde left prison a certain American journalist offered him a thousand pounds for a two hours' interview on the subject of his prison experience. The offer is said to have been communicated to Wilde, and Wilde is understood to have replied, with some hauteur, that he was astonished that such a proposal "should be placed before a gentleman." This was very fine talk, and it has been widely applauded by Wilde's admirers. I happen to know, however, that within three months of his release Wilde regretted bitterly that he had not closed with the American gentleman's proposition. At the time the offer was made Wilde knew that he had eight hundred pounds behind him, and he had been given to understand that large sums of money would be subscribed for him by his troop of admiring friends outside. The eight hundred pounds were there, right enough, but the mammoth subscription, or whip round, resulted in the collection of little more than a hundred pounds, the major portion of which was contributed by Frank Harris.

Wilde believed, also, that on his release he would find plenty of editors and publishers waiting for him, with hope in their eyes and fat cheques in their hands, and that he would be able to pick and choose among them in the matter of placing anything he might choose to say or write. Here again, however, he was mistaken; nobody deemed it worth while to make a bid for a Wilde book or a Wilde play, and he went to France commissionless.

As the beautiful Berneval weeks slipped away with the beautiful Berneval money, he began to have twinges of anxiety. He knew his world well and he knew that his world could do nothing for him. He had discovered, likewise, to his amazement, that Oscar Wilde, even with two years' hard labour to his credit, was not in any large sense marketable whether from a journalistic or a literary point of view. It was the general feeling of being "out of it" which spurred him on to build up the "Ballad of Reading Gaol." I know for a fact that he made offers to be interviewed for much less than a thousand pounds to the editors of various newspapers in England and America, but no one came near him. All he could manage to do for himself was to get certain letters printed in the *Daily Chronicle,* and for these, of course, he received nothing in the way of remuneration; so that the "Ballad of Reading Gaol" became important to him in a double sense.

He had taken the line that he was still an artist and too securely placed in his art to condescend to "low interviewing." He also felt that his one chance of getting back into something approximating to public favour was to produce some sort of a work of sustained and supreme power. This is why the "Ballad of Reading Gaol" is so long and so good. Wilde put all he knew and all he could into it. He even went to what was for him the fearful and unthinkable length of truckling somewhat to the more ordinary human sentiments in the tone of the poem, and avoided, as far as he could, those idiosyncrasies of Wilde the verse-maker which had always provoked the expostulation of the critics and the contempt or laughter of the general public. As we have seen, the "Ballad of Reading Gaol" was completed at Naples. I believe that Wilde was satisfied with every word of it. He had written to certain of his friends in England pooh-poohing it and pretending that it was in the manner of Sims; but he knew perfectly well that fifty Sims rolled into one would not have produced such a poem, and his self-deprecations were intended to soften his abandonment of the superior point of view rather than to express what he really felt. Having finished the poem, the next thing was to sell it. His thoughts turned to America, the land of hope and glory, and the land which had evolved that never-to-be-forgotten live journalist with his thousand pounds for an interview. Wilde solemnly forwarded the "Ballad of Reading Gaol" to a New York paper, the name of which wild horses shall not drag out of me, and proffered it for dollars, and the New York paper proceeded solemnly to erect an everlasting monument to its own stupidity by promptly returning the MS. So that for the two or three months

the "Ballad of Reading Gaol" was kicking about
in the world, with nobody to publish it. In the
meantime Wilde had gone to Paris, and he was
there sought out by the late Leonard Smithers, a
publisher who had done a great deal for Beardsley,
Dowson, and a number of quaint "geniuses" whose
names are now forgotten, and who had also published an unexpurgated edition of "Burton's Arabian Nights." Smithers took Wilde out to dinner,
produced an immediate handful of louis, and told
him that he was prepared to publish anything that
he cared to write. The "Ballad of Reading Gaol"
was raked out of a drawer and handed to Smithers,
and Smithers published it in England in February,
1898. The first edition consisted of eight hundred
copies at two-and-sixpence, with thirty copies on
Japanese vellum. Six further editions were called
for in twelve or fourteen months, and Smithers sent
from time to time various useful cheques for royal-
ties. I believe that he also purchased the book
rights of Wilde's plays, but that was the end of his
great publishing schemes for Oscar Wilde, for
Wilde produced nothing out of which a book could
be made after the "Ballad." I may note that two
or three years after Wilde's death Smithers, who
by this time had fallen upon somewhat evil days,
called on me and told me that he had drawings and,

if I remember rightly, plates for producing the "Harlot's House" in a very sumptuous and decorative form. The drawings were by Miss Althea Giles, and seemed to me to be very fine. With a view of giving both Miss Giles and Smithers a lift, I and a friend of mine put up the money Smithers required to go on with the publication. The "Harlot's House" had never been published in a book, though it had appeared in some obscure periodical. It did not occur to me that there could be any objection to Smithers publishing the book, which is a trifle in itself, and no more than thirty-six lines long. However, the next I heard about it was that Ross had stepped in, in his capacity of "literary executor," and stopped the publication. Ross did this without so much as referring to me in the matter, though, as far as I knew, we were on terms of friendship at the time. I suppose this is an instance of what Mr. Sherard calls "keeping a level commercial head in looking after Wilde's estate!"

CHAPTER XI

IN 1905 there was given to the world with a great flourish of trumpets a book entitled "De Profundis," which purported to be a work by Oscar Wilde. To this book Robert Ross supplied the preface. It will be necessary for us to examine this preface very thoroughly. Ross commences by explaining that for a long time curiosity had been expressed about the manuscript of "De Profundis," "which was known to be in my possession, the author having mentioned the existence to many other friends."

Presuming that Wilde mentioned the existence of this MS. to any of his other friends, I very much doubt whether he ever explained to them the nature of its contents. He no more dared do this than he dared have attempted to publish it, for he knew perfectly well that if he had told many other friends, whispers of his vileness and duplicity would have been sure to get round to me, and there might have been an end of my friendship and an end of my gifts.

At our first meeting after his release Wilde told me that he had "a hideous confession to make." He said that while he was in prison he had been told that I was no longer loyal to him and that I had expressed contempt for his sufferings. He said that he knew now that this was not true, but that it had preyed on his mind, and he had allowed it to anger him to such an extent that he had written me a very fierce and abominable letter and had it forwarded by Ross. I told him that I had a recollection of having received a copy of some such letter (not the letter itself) from Ross and with it a covering letter from Ross in which he said how sorry he was to have to send Wilde's letter, but that Wilde was apparently more or less out of his mind in consequence of the treatment he had received in prison, and was disposed to quarrel with everybody, and that he (Ross) hoped that I should take no notice of what he was sending. I threw the copy of Wilde's letter into the fire and I wrote to Ross to tell him to mind his own business, and to point out that if Wilde had anything to say to me he could say it in his own handwriting. So that when Wilde opened up his "hideous confession" I naturally thought that he was referring to the letter Ross had sent me, and I said: "My dear Oscar, I never read more than three or four lines of the wretched thing. I gathered that it was an ill-tempered letter and threw it into the fire. Don't let us talk any more about it. I quite understand how you must have felt, but it is all over now and there is nothing more to be said." It struck me, at the moment, as curious that Wilde should be wanting to make confessions as to having written a letter which he knew I had received, but I had no wish to pursue unpleasant matters, and the conversation dropped. From that day forward, though he was continually in my company and continually accepting kindnesses at my hand, he never breathed a single word about unpleasant letters or secret manuscripts or anything of the kind. It has been suggested by people who wish to make out that I had a copy of "De Profundis" sent to me in Wilde's lifetime that the letter which I received through Ross and burned was, in fact, "De Profundis," but this cannot be so, for the very simple reason that "De Profundis" is a fifty-thousand-word manuscript, whereas the letter I burned covered only several sides of ordinary letter paper in Ross's handwriting. I fail to see how Wilde's position is in the least degree improved even if it were granted that I had received a copy of the "De Profundis" manuscript; but, as a fact, I did not receive it.

Ross goes on to tell us that Wilde had instructed

him to publish "De Profundis." Those instructions, Mr. Ross tells us, were contained in a letter
from Wilde written to him, obviously from prison.
Part of this letter Mr. Ross has published in "De
Profundis," but he omitted the passages which gave
him the actual instructions. I should have much
liked to have seen these, for they might have thrown
some light on Wilde's action in leaving behind him
in the hands of others a posthumous libel on a man
who had been his friend up to and during his prison
period, and to whom he afterwards turned for
assistance and refuge.

It was not till "De Profundis" was announced
to be forthcoming by the press that I ever knew
that Wilde had left behind him an unpublished
manuscript of any sort or kind. When I learnt
that there was a manuscript and that it was to
be published under the editorship of Ross I was
very much astonished. Wilde had never spoken
to me of any manuscript which would be long
enough to make a book; neither had Ross, and
neither had anybody else. I was so astonished
that I went round to see Ross, who at that time
kept a picture shop in Ryder Street. I said to
him: "What is all this about an unpublished manuscript by Wilde? There is no such manuscript."
He said: "Oh, yes, there is." I said: "Then why

have you not told me of it before? and why did Wilde not tell me of it?" Ross said: "I wanted to keep it as a surprise." This struck me as being rather strange, and I said: "Wilde was hard up and keen on selling anything that he could get rid of. Why should he not have published it himself?" Ross replied: "He didn't do that because the MS. consists of a long letter. It contains a lot of disagreeable writing about you and other people, but I have cut this out, and what is left makes a nice little book." I said that it seemed a very extraordinary thing that nobody should have heard of this before, but Ross assured me that he would publish nothing that would hurt Wilde's reputation and that the book would do him good, and there the matter ended. When "De Profundis" was published there was not a word to indicate that it had been addressed to me and not to Ross at all, and the opposite deduction is one which the reader of the preface may fairly draw. For example, Ross quotes Wilde as saying that the privilege of writing to Ross at great length was one for which he was grateful to the Governor of the prison. Moreover, this impression still remains. Holbrooke Jackson, in his book "The Eighteen-Nineties" (published 1913), writes of Wilde: "During his imprisonment he wrote 'De Profundis' in the form of a long letter to his friend Robert Ross." "De Profundis" was published in 1895, and I never knew till 1912—seventeen years later, when the Ransome case was toward—that it was really addressed to me and that the unpublished parts were still in existence and amounted to more than half of the whole manuscript. Still less did I dream that the unpublished moiety—as any reader of the reports of the Ransome trial can see for himself—contained gross libels on myself or that the British Museum authorities had kindly consented to accept it as a present to the nation without so much as consulting any of us. I leave the facts as I have set them forth to the judgment of the public.

The existence of the "De Profundis" manuscript forces us to one of two alternatives: Wilde, according to Ross, wished it to be published and gave it to Ross with a view to publication, never afterwards changing his mind on the subject or desiring that the manuscript should be destroyed. In that case he has exhibited a perfidy which is without parallel in history, inasmuch as for three years after leaving prison and right up till the time of his death he professed to be my devoted and attached friend and accepted in friendship what I was very pleased to give in friendship.

The other alternative is that, on leaving prison

and finding that he had been misinformed as to my attitude toward him, he repented the writing of this manuscript and intended it to be destroyed, but failed to cancel his instructions.

While the Ransome case was pending I wrote Ross a letter setting out the facts stated above, namely, that I had never any idea that "De Profundis" was a letter addressed to me or that it had any connection with the letter which Ross had sent me in 1897. I also informed him of Wilde's solitary reference to the letter, which I have previously referred to. I expected Ross to give me some reply by way of explanation, but received none. I consider that, in view of the circumstances, he might have taken the opportunity of ridding the memory of his friend of what, in the absence of such an explanation, must be regarded by all fair-minded persons as an act of cowardly and abominable treachery. As it is, seeing how zealous an adherent of Wilde Ross is, I am forced to the conclusion that Wilde was playing the Judas with me all the time we were together at Naples and all the time that he was lunching and dining and "meeting his difficulties" at my expense in Paris.

Before proceeding to refute charges brought against me at the Ransome trial, based on Wilde's posthumous libel, I should like to enquire whether

it can be considered proper, either on literary
grounds or on grounds of public policy, that a book
like "De Profundis" should be given to the world
at all. Mr. Ransome tells us that the book is composed of passages from a long letter the complete
publication of which would be impossible in this
generation. "The passages were selected and put
together," he adds, "by Mr. Robert Ross, with a
skill that it is impossible sufficiently to admire."
Quite so. But it can be demonstrated out of the
text that Mr. Ross's selectings and puttings-
together have, in the net result, entirely deceived
the public, not only with regard to the nature and
intentions of "De Profundis" as a book, but also
with regard to Wilde's own character and his attitude towards his own misfortune. What right has
Mr. Ross or any other person, no matter how skilled,
to indulge in this kind of literary liberty? Despite
what Wilde himself said to the contrary, it is always
important that we should know as much as is possible to be known about any man who sets up to
teach us, and especially is this so in the case of an
author like Wilde, whose whole writings amount
really to a sort of personal statement. Mr. Ross
recognises this much, because in his version of "De
Profundis" he offers no samples of Wilde the
vituperative spitter-out of venom or of Wilde the

braggart and vain boaster, such as appear in the reports of the Ransome trial, but shows us simply the Wilde who weeps profusely and swears that he has turned saint. "And I do this," says Ross, in his preface, "hoping that my efforts will give many readers a different impression of the witty and delightful writer." The "different impression" has obviously resulted. Wilde emerges from the mire a gracious, suffering, forgiving, magnanimous figure. The extracts from Wilde's own manuscript, read and relied on by the counsel for the defendant in the Ransome trial, prove him to have been nothing of the kind, and, for that matter, the direct opposite. On literary grounds alone we are surely entitled to protest against such a dangerous violation of the normal editorial function. If we are to take "De Profundis" for an approved precedent, a literary executor is justified in treating a dead man's inedited manuscripts in such a way that he is made to say only half of what he really did say, and so made to appear the direct opposite of what he really was. On public grounds one is entitled to protest even more strongly. We have, in Wilde, a person of careless and vicious life, whose talents were always carelessly and at times viciously employed. Such a man was almost, in the nature of things, bound to come to a miserable and degraded end. Wilde ended up in prison for his offences, and if he had really repented and had really written "De Profundis," as published without the suppressed portion, and lived out the rest of his life in a decent way, it would have been possible and proper for us to forgive and forget a great deal; but, unless he has maligned himself most madly, he never did repent, and it is certain that "De Profundis," as published, does not represent his sentiments or his nature. The result has been that a false and specious glamour has been put upon the aim and trend of Wilde's life and writings, and very generally the *apologia* contained in the bowdlerised "De Profundis" is regarded as a sufficient *"Apologia pro Vita sua."*

Commenting on the reading of the unpublished parts of "De Profundis" at the Ransome trial, the *Outlook* said:

"Those who heard its unpublished portions . . . fall from the lips of the learned junior counsel for the defence, or even those who had to be content with such portions their newspapers gave them, had the unusual experience of sharing the privileges reserved for posterity. They have added to their knowledge of the last prose work of Oscar Wilde; indeed, they have gained their first true knowledge of the form in which it left his pen. They know

that it begins 'Dear Bosie,' and ends 'Your affectionate friend, Oscar Wilde,' but it is not always
either friendly or affectionate. They know that
there are parts—about meals and the influenza and
the respect that is due to a great artist—'and especially such an artist as I am'—that are not an expression of the mood which gave to the world the
well-known parts about Christ. They have learned,
for the first time, that some parts have been taken
and that other parts have been left—to the nation.
In the parts that have been taken, and strung, like
beads, on a new string, to form the book the world
knows, they have learned that the 'you' addressed
is not general and impersonal, but the friend who,
whatever the rights and wrongs of last week, has
at least written poetry that is better than Wilde's
own, in spite of the mood of scolding superiority in
which the letter seems to have begun."

It has been suggested that the article from which
this passage is an extract was written by my friend
T. W. H. Crosland and inserted in *The Outlook*
through the influence of George Wyndham. Anybody who is acquainted with London journalism
knows that Mr. Crosland has had nothing to do
with *The Outlook* since he resigned the Literary
Editorship of that journal in 1902; and Mr. Wyndham ceased to have any interest in the paper some

months later. The author of the article is, so far as I am aware, entirely unknown to me, and, in any case, it was not written by my desire or inspiration.

I have already referred to certain charges against me, in support of which passages from the unpublished parts of "De Profundis" were put to me at the Ransome trial, and shown how preposterous they are. I had an opportunity, at the time of the Ransome trial, of reading a copy of the manuscript with great care; and I say advisedly that, in so far as it concerns me, I had great difficulty in finding a single statement which could not be demonstrated to be utterly, deliberately and ridiculously false. If Mr. Robert Ross will remove his embargo I am open to print the whole of such portions of "De Profundis," word for word and line for line, with plain demonstrations of the absolute malice and contempt for the truth that Wilde has exhibited right through the piece. As it is, at present I am prevented from quoting or even from paraphrasing any portions owing to the legal steps taken by Mr. Ross. But, in order that it may never be suggested that I fear or admit the charges brought against me in the Ransome trial, and to clear myself from them, I propose to deal with the more serious of them (not already dealt with in Chapter VIII) as assertions of fact and not even by way of paraphrase of the precious

MS. I should have preferred to put these charges into Wilde's own words, and so have given my posthumous libeller every opportunity of couching his attack in his own way and with all the master's skill. But Mr. Ross has prevented this by obtaining an injunction against me. I do not think, however, that either he or the law can prevent me from dealing with allegations of fact made against me in cross-examination *quâ* allegations of fact.

I have already referred to the falseness of Wilde's charge that I hampered his work, and that when I was by he was sterile. I had to meet the charge, in particular, that when he was pressed to deliver "The Ideal Husband" he had to wait till I was away and then got on famously. When I returned, "all work had to be abandoned." This assertion is wantonly wrong. When Wilde was in working mood he worked and I never attempted to take him away from it. The play was read to me scene by scene and line by line, and so far from my having delayed its completion I materially assisted it. If one were disposed to be flippant and to admit that Wilde gives a correct description of our daily programme at St. James' Place, one might enquire why—if he found it impossible to work in the atmosphere of his own quiet and peaceful household and found it equally impossible to work at St.

James' Place because of my interruptions—he never locked the door of St. James' Place, never contrived to be out, and never omitted to send me telegrams of enquiry and letters of pleasant rebuke if I happened to miss calling upon him. Wilde was too keen an artist to allow anything or anybody to come between him and what he would call a realisable mood. The truth is that he would begin a work with great zeal and fury and apply himself to it and to the contemporaneous consumption of cigarettes and whiskies till he became utterly exhausted. As a rule, he completed what he had begun in a series of spurts and with periods of easy donothingness between whiles. On the other hand, there were occasions when he got stuck, and he got stuck over more than one of his plays. This is merely to say that he was like any other artist; to blame me for it is childish or lunatic—whichever you will. Wilde began "The Sphinx"—a work of which he was inordinately proud—when he was little more than twenty years of age: he was thirty-eight before he finished it, and then, apparently, he had to call in no less a poet than Robert Harborough Sherard, author of "Whispers," to help him out with rhymes ending with "ar." Sherard tells us with great pomp and pride that he suggested "nenuphar"—a substantive of Greek origin, which had been worn to

death by precious poets before either Wilde or
Sherard was born, but the sudden and glorious discovery of which by Sherard appears to have trans-
ported them both into the seventh heaven.

It is absolutely untrue that my mother, the
Dowager Marchioness of Queensberry, ever informed Wilde at Bracknell that I was "vain," or
"wrong about money." My mother has never been
in the habit of discussing the characters of those
near and dear to her with anybody, much less with
comparative strangers. On his own showing,
Wilde scarcely knew me at this period, and on the
only occasion he was at my mother's house near
Bracknell there were a dozen other guests staying
in the house, and his conversations with my mother
would be of the very slightest, and amount, so far
as she was concerned, to the merest civilities when
they met at lunch or dinner. My mother is still
alive and, whether at Bracknell or anywhere else,
she did not say to Wilde what he professes she said.
It is the same with the charge that our residence
at Goring, where I was well known, cost him a fabulous sum. If this is so, seeing that we shared
expenses of the Goring establishment, Wilde appears to have let me off exceedingly cheaply for
my half-share; for I do not recollect that it cost me
more than twenty or thirty pounds a month, exclud-

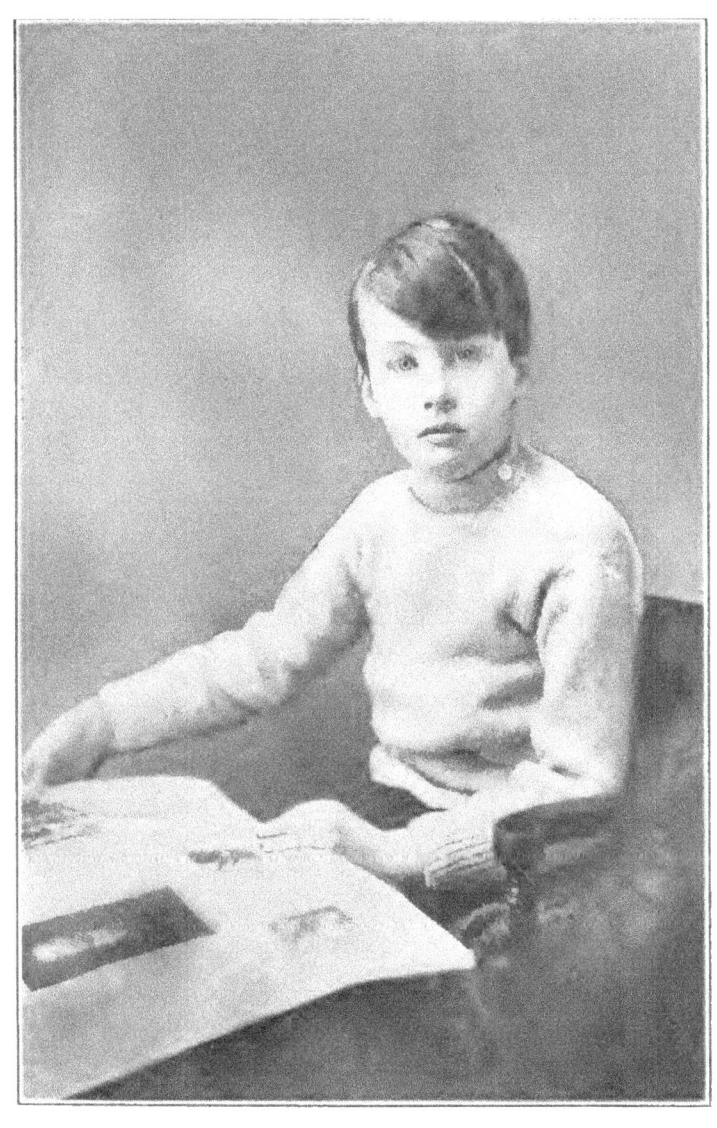

RAYMOND WILFRID SHOLTO DOUGLAS, ONLY CHILD OF LORD
ALFRED DOUGLAS, BORN 17TH NOVEMBER, 1902
(AGED NINE IN THE PHOTOGRAPH)

ing the rent, of which I never heard, inasmuch as Wilde professed that the house had been lent to him by a well-known member of the Peerage. If thirteen hundred pounds were spent by Wilde at Goring during those three months, all I can say is that at least twelve hundred must have gone in rent; for we lived very simply there, and there were no restaurants into which one could be lured to a meal which would cost "a whole sovereign." So Goring won't do, any more than the five thousand pounds worth of ortolans and *Perrier Jouet*. One other small matter and I shall have done with this part of the subject.

I deny emphatically that I gambled and lost at Algiers and expected him to pay my losses. At the time Wilde and I went to Algiers together I had just come into some money, and I took a suite of rooms at the best hotel in the place. Wilde stayed there with me, and I paid the hotel bill myself. There was not, so far as I am aware, a *tripot* or other gambling place—much less a Casino—in Algiers at that period, so that neither of us could gamble even if we had wished to. Wilde returned to London before me for business reasons; but the business was entirely his own and had nothing to do with me, and I lent him fifteen pounds to pay his fare home. By some aberration or other he actually returned me this money, paying a cheque for the amount into my account in London. In all the literature of the subject, that is to say, in all the pass-books, banking accounts, business and private letters, and so forth, that are in existence or ever did exist, this is the sole and only instance of Wilde ever paying a sum of money to me; whereas it could be demonstrated out of the same documents that I paid a very great many sums to Wilde. In the safe seclusion of Reading Gaol he sits, tearfully penitent, and remembers that fifteen pounds, which, no doubt, loomed up in his memory like a shot-tower. He catches at it, gleefully, and uses it as a peg on which to hang a false, preposterous, lying story about meeting my gambling debts in a place where there is no gambling. At the back of his mind he knew that nothing of the kind ever occurred, yet the fifteen pound payment might have lent colour to the statement if it came to be investigated after my death. And that was all the colour he had for his pretty statement.

I have no wish to be uncharitable to this man who, doubtless, suffered, and suffered severely. Nobody could read the complete "De Profundis" without perceiving that imprisonment destroyed Wilde's moral fibre and crushed his spirit to such an extent that he became a sort of Mrs. Gummidge who felt everything "more than you do." I am forced to think—and, to be quite frank, I try to think—that Wilde cannot have been mentally responsible when he wrote this stupid and abominable manuscript. That I am not alone in my opinion of what confinement and bitter discipline were doing for him will be evident from the following letter which I received from a close friend of Ross's at the time when Wilde was supposed to be angry with me. The letter is dated from a house which was at that time occupied by Ross and the writer of the letter.

"My Dear Bosie,

"Your letter distresses me, for I can say so little to comfort you and I would do all I can. You will know by this time that I had seen Oscar before I received your letter. I saw him on Saturday, 30th November, the very day you wrote, and I only got your letter to-day, Tuesday. You must not think that I do not know what Oscar's change towards you must be to you, but Robbie will tell you that from the very first I never believed that it was more than a passing delirium of gaol moral fever. I naturally minimised to you and Robbie, when I wrote, the horrors of the general prison surroundings, but I have seen them,

and am confirmed in my belief that no man like
Oscar who is subject to them can be considered
capable of exercising his ordinary mental or moral
faculties. What he says now no more expresses
his proper natural feelings than do the ravings of
a man in delirium. I am certain that his mind *has*
very much suffered, but I think from what I have
heard of him before, and what I have seen of him,
that he is better; and I think that he is conscious
that he must make efforts to prevent his mind
suffering more, because he was so very anxious to
get some rather drudging mental work to do, in
order to occupy and, in a sort of way, discipline
his mind. In former interviews he spoke of you
just as a lunatic or a man in delirium does of the
people they love best, but the other day he did not
do so; he merely complained of some letter which
you had written to him or to the Governor (I suppose of Wandsworth) which he had heard of but
was not allowed to see. I told him that I was certain that you would write no more. He has to be
talked to as a person very slowly recovering from
delirium. I could not have said anything to distress him. Just think, he has only one half-hour in
the awful weeks of hideous prison life. You must
try to show the love which I know you have for
him, by the most difficult of all ways—*waiting*."

There may be—and probably is—a good deal to
be said for the view herein set forward, and it
would be inhuman not to make all necessary allow-
ances.   But we are still left face to face with the
unchallengeable fact that Wilde was sane enough
when he came out of prison; that his health was
on the whole improved by his sojourn there; and
that for three years he kept up his friendship with
me, and lived to a great extent on my bounty; and
that he never said a single word about the disgrace-
ful document which Mr. Ross has so generously be-
stowed upon the nation.

CHAPTER XII

THE law as to property in letters appears to be in a very confused and amazing condition. Letters, though lightly penned by most people and considered to be of trifling importance, are nearly always far more important than they look. If I had been cautious and worldly-wise I suppose that the letters which I wrote to Oscar Wilde or, at any rate, those which were produced by favour of Ross at the Ransome trial, would never have been written. The fact that they were written, however, cannot be denied, and, for many reasons, I am not sorry that they were brought up against me. I knew that some such letters existed, and I was told before the trial came on that they would be produced and that they would ruin me. Well, to the great consternation and amazement of the parties immediately concerned I went into the witness-box and "faced the music," and I was not ruined. By a coincidence, it happened that I had various difficulties of litigation

round about the time of the Ransome trial, and
rumour had it that those troubles were in some way
bound up with the Wilde affair. As a fact, they
had nothing to do with it, and were quite indepen-
dent of it, and even the endeavour to create a public
impression that my wife had left me because of the
Ransome trial proved utterly futile. The unfortunate differences between myself and Lady Alfred
Douglas arose out of matters of settlements and
the education of our child, and, lest my enemies
should lay the flattering unction to their souls that
they have succeeded in separating us, I may mention here and now that my wife and I are no longer
at variance and that our reconciliation was brought
about by our two selves after the trial and not
before it. In the witness-box I made no bones about
condemning the two letters of mine which were
raked up to show that I had a bad influence over
Wilde's mind. I shall not attempt to justify them
here, and I shall not abate my opinion of them one
jot or tittle. They are letters which I am ashamed
to have written and which I ought to have a good
deal too much sense to write. They have not been
printed in the press and I shall not reproduce them
here, any more than I would think of reproducing
similar letters written by Wilde and his friends. I
do not think, however, that any man of the world

who perused them could fail to recognise that they were letters written more or less in a jocular spirit, and that they were plainly not the letters of the kind of person some people have been gracious enough to wish to make me out. At school, the universities, and even in clubs, men who are not considered by any means wicked men make jokes, exchange jokes, and tell stories which, one takes it, would very much shock Mr. Justice Darling if they happened to come to his polite ears. There are persons of the highest positions in all walks of life—not even forgetting the immaculate and stainless profession of the law—who in their day and generation could swap coarse jokes with any stable-boy, and who, over their wine, are not above indulging in a trifle of witty obscenity, even yet. Everybody knows this, and nobody pretends that it is otherwise, or that it is ever likely to be otherwise. The only place where you get such a pretence is in the law courts, when Counsel wishes to "eviscerate" somebody. The pretence was well kept up at the Ransome trial by all parties concerned and as I have said before, I do not in the least complain but am rather glad than otherwise. For the improper is obviously the improper wherever you encounter it, and there is no reason why my impropriety should be extenuated while the next man's is punished. I

punished myself for my offences against decency
and good taste by standing up and having them read
out to me twenty years after they were written. I
could have run away from them if I had wished to,
but I stood my ground and took my gruel with a
short spoon. The result has been exactly what one
was entitled to expect that it would be. I have not
lost a single friend or come across a single cold
shoulder as the result of Mr. Ross's letter-preserv-
ing charitableness. My cousin, the late Right Honourable George Wyndham, M.P., than whom no
more honourably-minded man existed, wrote to me
immediately after the trial and told me that he
had followed it closely, and that nothing had happened which was to make any difference between
himself and myself, and he added that, not only
in his opinion but in the opinion of many persons
with whom he had talked, I had been abominably
treated. Of course, it is preposterous to say that
my influence over Wilde was a bad influence. If
the letters produced to prove it prove anything at
all, they prove, rather, that Wilde's influence over
me was a bad one, and a very bad one at that. Any
one who knows me must be well aware that, when it
came to the question of his ultimate vices, such influence as I had over him was on the side of goodness
and decency rather than otherwise. In all his cun-

ning, overweening and merciless desire to damage and destroy me, Wilde could never find it in his heart to set down the last unthinkable lie. He knew that if he did that he would be blankly sinning against the Holy Ghost, and, hate me as he would, and rage and rage as he would, he could not bring himself to take the terrible risks. Nowhere in all this outpouring of hate does he dare to come out with the accusation which would put me outside the pale of social possibility. That he was quite willing to have shouted that accusation out at the top of his voice if there had been the slightest ground for it is only too evident from the general drift of what he has to say. If by a deft ambiguity he can get in the hint that will hurt me without going the length of the rankest perjury he gets it in. It is plain on every showing that our friendship was a harmless and proper friendship and that our life together was harmlessly, if, perhaps, somewhat extravagantly, lived; and two things have always to be remembered: first, that during our friendship, whether despite me or otherwise, Wilde did undoubtedly produce the best of his plays and the finest of his poems, indeed, the only poem which is likely to live; while, during the same friendship, I, for my part, produced the bulk of the poetry contained in the "City of the Soul." There is nothing in any of the work produced by Wilde during the time that we were together of which he need be ashamed, and there is nothing in the "City of the Soul" of which I need be ashamed. On the contrary, Wilde's reputation, in so far as it is a pure literary reputation, has been largely built up on the work to which I refer, whereas it is largely by my own work during that period that I shall stand or fall so far as posterity is concerned. How dare people assail and defame an association of this kind? I print below two letters which were sent to me by Mr. George Wyndham immediately after the Ransome trial.

I leave the parties concerned to make the best they can of an outside opinion, and to meditate with what gratification they may on their "base thing."

34 James Street
Buckingham Gate
Thursday 24ᵃ

My dear Bosie
I daresay a Tip will be acceptable. so I send you a cheque for 90£ as I have some spare cash. have not heard of or from you for ever so long. don't be so foolish as to think any more about the stuff of my speaking to you about
yours

Handwriting. if you take
trouble you can improve it
very much & it is a very.
important things Writing
a good hand & also shews
very much the state one is
_in_ →

I have been to Monte Carlo
& won some money & then lost
it all again. but did not
do any harm & as it was
horribly cold
there

I came back to Paris
where I stopped for about
ten days. & then hope I
am going back for a
fortnight as I have been
taking some lessons in
French before the _advent_
where they are their _feet_

I am rather thinking
of taking another globe
trot & if I go shall
start alone

the 15th of April as some friends
of mine are then going To
America & I should have
their company & then go
on To Benarass To look
after some property I
have there. which is getting
on well. if I do that I
should go on perhaps To
Japan & come home by
India. when I could go &
look up Percys up
　　　Yours affecte father
　　　　Queensberry

22. iv. 13.

My dear Bosie
Since writing you
a matter - of - fact letter
this morning I see, by the
Evening Papers, that you
failed to get a verdict
in your libel action. Don't
take that to heart. I

alters nothing that
matters.

Your family have
known, for 20 years,
that you had the great
misfortune — as I think —
of accepting, when you
were very young, the
influence of a clever
brain that took delight
in perversity.

I write this merely
to say that the result of
this lawsuit does not
alter my view.

Your affecte cousin

George Wyndham

CHAPTER XIII

MY LETTERS TO LABOUCHERE

THAT the late Henry Labouchere was a good deal of a blackguard is well known, but he was one of those blackguards who managed to get into the House of Commons and, as impudence was a gift with him, he made some reputation there. When Gladstone proposed to give him a Cabinet appointment, however, Queen Victoria calmly drew her pen through his name. Gladstone gasped, but Labouchere did not become a Minister of the Crown. Labby's strength lay in his money. A poorer rogue would not have been tolerated, even in the House of Commons. And Labby's weakness was *Truth*—the paper, not the abstraction. Labouchere always made a great point of running *Truth* in the interests of public morality. For quack doctors, begging-letter writers, and certain classes of bookmakers and money-lenders he had, invariably, abundant stripes; but for the very big fish Henry Labouchere had a confirmed respect and was most careful to say nothing about them and do nothing to them—unless they happened to fall, when he would rush in and deliver a few kicks. It is not astonishing that as soon as Oscar Wilde came to grief Henry Labouchere should have hastened to put in his bit of kicking. While Wilde was flaunting himself about town and "going strong," Labby found it convenient to let him alone, even though "there were rumours"—and *Truth* was nothing if not an investigator of rumours. In his hey-dey, therefore, Labby would say no word that was evil of Wilde, though he poked fun at him. But the moment Mr. Justice Wills hands out two years' hard labour and Wilde is down and past mortal chance of getting up again, forth comes Labby, with his silly little patent-leather boots and his dirty little dagger, and Wilde is kicked and stabbed without mercy. Incidentally, too, Labby took the opportunity to refer to me as a "young scoundrel" and to accuse me of deserting my friend in his trouble. I wrote and pointed out that, so far from deserting Wilde, I was the one and only friend of his who remained faithful to him after his arrest, and visited him daily in prison, and when he was up at Bow Street Police Station; and I went on to express my opinion of the mean and unnecessary venom of Labby's attacks on a man who was down and unable to defend himself. It is characteristic of Labouchere that, while he was too much of a coward to print my letters in full, and was content to publish only that part of one of them in which I defended myself against his charge of deserting my friend, he was careful to preserve them. Eighteen years after they were written *Truth* turned up in court with them to be used against me in a matter with which *Truth* was not in any way concerned. I presume that they were produced under subpœna, though how their existence became known to Mr. Ransome remains a mystery. With that fine sense of what is fitting which distinguishes him, Mr. Justice Darling explained that the people who have kept and produced my letters are not to be blamed, "inasmuch," said his lordship, "as they are only doing what they are paid to do," which is somewhat cryptic, but is possibly meant to be funny. However, I really do not care "tuppence" who treasures these letters of mine. The only point is that somehow it seems un-English and unsportsmanlike. As for the letters themselves, they failed entirely in the object to which they were put by Ransome's lawyers. I cannot find that it was thought wise to print extracts from them in the newspapers at the time of the trial. And, as I have not got possession of them and am apparently not entitled to possession of them, I cannot print them here, even if I were disposed to do so. I know what is in them, however, and there is no reason why I should not summarise them. The letters contain the stock arguments of those apologists for the perversion to which Wilde was addicted which were current at the time. They point out that vice of this character was rampant in the West End of London and at certain public schools and universities, and that Labby had not said a word about it in his wonderful paper—*Truth.* The letters also quote or epitomise sundry medical and scientific views on the subject. That is all. What I had to say I said plainly and without beating about the bush, and, while I should not write such letters to-day, there is nothing about them which is greatly to my discredit. During the whole time of the trial there sat in court the author of the following statement: "It is a matter of common observation among physiologists that where a child is born to a couple in which the woman has the much stronger nature and a great mental superiority over the father, the chances are that the child will develop at certain critical periods in his career an extraordinary attraction towards persons of its own sex. This fact is one of Nature's mysteries. Those who believe in a Divine Creation of the world should reverently

bow their heads before what they cannot understand and ought to take to be a divine dispensation.
At any rate, the wisdom of Nature may be pre-
sumed greater than that of the Ecclesiastical
Courts."

There is nothing in my letters to Labouchere
which can in the least compare with the foregoing
passage, which I take from "The Life of Oscar
Wilde," by Robert Harborough Sherard. Sherard's
"Life," like Ransome's "Critical Study," is published broadcast and under everybody's nose, and
both of them, as we have seen, contain their individual views of Wilde's vices.

CHAPTER XIV

IN pursuance of what I conceived to be my duty towards Wilde at the time he was in prison, I wrote the Labouchere letters and a good deal of similar matter which was not printed. My argument was not that Wilde had wrongfully been convicted, and not that what he did was to be counted to his credit, or even to be approved, but merely that there were scientific and medical grounds for supposing that he was not responsible for his actions in this regard, and that, in any case, the punishment meted out to him seemed unnecessarily and brutally severe. I do not know that I have changed my opinion to this day. It is unthinkable that a sane person could flounder into the loathsome depths in which Wilde was taken red-handed; particularly is it unthinkable in respect of a man of Wilde's culture and social surroundings.

That he was sane enough in other regards cannot be doubted, but I do not think there can be any question as to his insanity on this particular point.

But this is as far as I go, and this is as far as any decently-minded person can go. I never went an inch further, and never intended to. I have already stated that after sentence was passed upon Wilde all Paris appeared to go off its head with regard to the scandal. Many absurd and unfounded pieces of gossip were published in the French newspapers, and some of these I took it upon myself to endeavour to refute. When it became known that I was in Paris, the interviewers flocked round me and wanted me to talk to them on all manner of silly matters. I declined to have anything to do with them in a general way, especially as I found that they were disposed to garble and exaggerate everything one might tell them. One fine morning, however, there called upon me a journalist with whom I had some acquaintance, who told me that he had been commissioned by the Editor of the *Revue Blanche* to get me to write an article on the Wilde affair in which my views should be set out definitely and finally, and thus put an end to the extraordinary stories which were being circulated in my name. I knew the *Revue Blanche* as a weekly literary journal of somewhat advanced opinions, and I thought that here was an excellent opportunity to say something that might be of use to Wilde. My difficulty was that, while I spoke French fluently, I did not feel that I had a sufficient command of style and so forth to write the article in French. My friend the journalist was very accommodating, however, and it was arranged between us that, with the knowledge of the Editor of the *Revue Blanche,* I was to write an article in English which would be translated into French and inserted in the paper over my name. I wrote the article and handed it to the representative of the *Revue,* for translation and publication. I stipulated for a proof in French, but the next I heard about the matter was that the article had appeared. The translator, whoever he was, simply took my article as a sort of peg, and hung on it a farrago of extremely vicious opinions, and even more vicious comparisons which I had never put forward, and which my own article certainly did not suggest. I complained to the Editor of the *Revue* at the time, but found myself unable to obtain any redress, and there was nothing more to be done. The French article passed almost unnoticed, inasmuch as the *Revue Blanche* had a very limited circulation, and I never heard another word about it until years after, when I was editing *The Academy.* In that paper I had occasion to write a paragraph about a journal called *The Freethinker,* which was edited by a Mr. Foote, and which made a sort of business of blasphemy. Mr. Foote was not pleased at what I said about him and, by way of retort, he translated a particularly nauseous passage from the *Revue Blanche* article, inserted it in his journal and accused me of being the author. I immediately issued a writ for libel against the proprietors of the *Freethinker,* and, after receiving the writ, Mr. Foote discovered that he had made a serious mistake and promptly apologised in the next issue of his paper. He did not even enter an appearance. I was content with my apology and allowed the action to lapse.

This is the whole truth about the *Revue Blanche* article. Though the *Revue* is now dead, the proprietor and editor are, I believe, still alive. If, as was contended in the Ransome trial, I wrote the article I am said to have written, or furnished the material for it, these gentlemen could easily have been produced to say so. But they were not brought forward as witnesses and were not even approached on the subject. Yet the article was put in at the trial and, though I said on oath in court what I now say here in print—and my assertion was not in the slightest degree shaken by cross-examination—Mr. Justice Darling persisted in reading aloud, and for the benefit of the jury, words which I had not written, and this in spite of my explanations and protest. There is no use in complaining, nor do I complain. I merely put it on record once for all, that the *Revue Blanche* article is not my article, and I am in no way responsible for it.

CHAPTER XV

I DO not think it is an exaggeration to say that from the day of Oscar Wilde's sentence in 1887 down to the Ransome trial in 1913 not a single week had passed over my head without some unpleasantness or other arising in consequence of my friendship with Oscar Wilde. Even before Wilde was sent to prison the trouble began. There was talk and gossip almost from the commencement of our acquaintanceship. This was largely set afoot by envious people. Wilde's friends could not brook that we should be so constantly together, and that I should—to use their own phrase —"monopolise" him.

In point of fact, I had no desire to monopolise him. It was simply impossible to shake him off. If I left him for a day he would seek me out and want to know where I had been and why I had not asked him to accompany me. If I went abroad he would follow me and either entreat me to return or sit down solemnly and wait my time. So continually were we together that our friendship became matter for public comment and was referred to in the newspapers. I do not say that I disliked all this, though it was certainly embarrassing and even annoying at times. In a sense, perhaps, I was rather flattered. I have always been fond of companionship, and Wilde was undoubtedly an entertaining companion when he liked. Besides which he was famous in a way, and it is not always unpleasant to go about with famous people, particularly when they happen to be very civil to one. It is a fact that Wilde could not bear me out of his sight. If we happened to be staying together and I went away for ten minutes without telling him where I was going, he would work himself up into a state of nervous apprehension and rouse a whole hotel with his enquiries.

I remember that when we were at a hotel in Algiers, I went out to make a purchase without mentioning to Wilde that I was going. On my return, half an hour later, I was met in the hall by a scared-looking *concierge,* who said: "Monsieur, you are back! *Votre papa* has been demanding to know where you were, with great noise, for the last hour!" Wilde happened to be descending the staircase at this precise moment and overheard what the man had said. The expression *"votre papa"* simply drove him to fury. He was always vain of his "youthful appearance" (though, as a matter of fact, he looked much older than his age), and he jumped to the conclusion that he was beginning to look old. He could not see that his anxious queries as to my whereabouts had set the hotel people thinking that he must stand in a parental relationship to the object of his solicitude. For myself, I was vastly amused and, for months after, if I wished to make Wilde fearfully angry, I had only to say *"votre papa."*

I may, perhaps, explain here that from the very beginning I always treated Wilde in the way I would treat any other friend of mine, that is to say, though I believed him to be a great man, I never had any awe of him, and I never flattered him. Not only so, but at times I made a great deal of fun of him, and there were occasions when he didn't relish it. For example, he had been talking to me and to other people at great length about Milton. Somebody in a paper had pointed out that certain of his sonnets had a Miltonic echo about them. He admitted that this was so, but said that what the critic called an echo was really an achievement, and that he had wilfully set himself to write sonnets like Milton's, which should be as good as Milton's. For several days his conversation turned in the same direction, and in the end I began to grow a little weary of the Milton-Wilde amalgamation, and told him that it was quite easy to write Miltonic sonnets, and that lots of people could do it besides Oscar Wilde. On leaving him that evening I wrote and posted to him the following sonnet, which, I need hardly say, was "writ sarcastic":

> Oscar! what though no brazen trumpet-call
> Of Fame hath called thee to the foremost van
> Of life's array, though not from man to man
> Thy name is bandied, though thy life seem small,
> Ignoble in men's eyes; the Lord of all,
> Who reads the heart and with his fearful fan
> Purges his floor, knows thy true talisman—
> A humble soul too near the ground to fall.
>
> Therefore, repine not if thy lot obscure
> Seeks quiet ways and walks not with the crowd:
> A kindly heart is more than laurel crown;
> A virtuous life builds thrones that will endure
> More surely than the Kingdoms of the proud
> And Thrift shall stand when Luxury falls down.

Wilde professed to take this "undergraduate effusion" seriously, and pronounced it to be "not bad, for an amateur." But we heard no more about Miltonic sonnets.

I mention these things, which are typical, so that the reader may be spared the conclusion that my friendship with Wilde was a smooth and treacly affair; for it was nothing of the kind. Indeed, we had many a tiff and many a disagreement, and I wrote no end of skits and letters to him, some of them not over civil; and that he remembered them and that they hurt him much more keenly than I had intended is shown by his references to "loathsome" and "brutal" letters received from me. Anything that displeased Wilde was loathsome, brutal, callous, coarse, and so forth. If I wrote and said:—

"MY DEAR OSCAR,

"I am afraid that I shall not be able to come round to lunch to-day as I am feeling a bit off colour,"

I could count on getting a reply in some such terms as:—

"I have received your callous note. If you are ill, surely you can say so without using coarse and vulgar expressions."

I took precious little notice of these missives and, when we met the next day, neither of us would refer to them.

As I have said, people gossipped about our friendship and exhibited a certain amount of jealousy of me; but I was not then, and never have been, disposed to allow third parties to interfere in my friendships. I have shown what happened when my own father attempted to make differences between us. The moment Wilde was sentenced things were made intolerable for me. Lying tales as to my indifference to his fate reached Wilde, and he was told that I was about to publish letters of his to his damage and my own monetary profit. The only letters of Wilde's I ever proposed to publish, in my life, were letters which contained sentiments that were to his credit, and even these I withdrew the moment I heard that he was supposed not to wish them printed. Not only was every effort made to embitter and estrange Wilde against me while he was in prison, but I was being continually assailed by impudent rogues who professed to have information and documents which it would be worth my while to buy. To these people I paid neither the smallest heed nor the smallest of monies. They never had a farthing from me, nor will they ever get one. I was threatened with "exposure" by pretty well all the crawling vermin of London and Paris for months after the trial. I knew there was nothing to expose, so that I was not particularly anxious; but seeing, as I had seen, what venom and villainy were capable of doing when they got fairly to work, I do not profess that these threats were pleasant reading of a morning at breakfast. Furthermore, my family were assailed in much the same way and, though they never allowed them-

LADY ALFRED DOUGLAS

selves to be victimised, they were not entirely delighted with the constant current of menace which
came their way.

In 1902 I married. It was a runaway match,
which neither myself nor my wife have ever repented. At once, however, the dastardly attentions
of the blackmailers, letter-sellers and information
mongers were directed to Lady Alfred. We lived
abroad for a considerable time and, though the
threats had been bad enough while we were away,
they assumed a double fury when we came to England. They have continued with greater or less
frequency ever since. The people who wanted
money to keep quiet have fallen off unappeased long
ago. But the kind and gentle souls who imagined
that Lady Alfred Douglas would be pleased to hear
"something dreadful" about her husband on an
anonymous postcard are still with us and crop up
from time to time as the spirit moves them. When
I took over the editorship of *The Academy,* in 1907,
the fun became fast and furious. We could not
review a book adversely in the paper without being
made the object of anonymous threats and abuse
with reference to Wilde, and what was going to be
done to us if we didn't look out. Persons on papers
at Oxford and Cambridge wrote paragraphs about
the Editor of *The Academy* containing veiled sug-

gestions as to the discreditable character of his former relations with Wilde, till we were compelled to
take legal proceedings; then they fell on their knees
and wept bitterly and spoke of their dying fathers
and apologised humbly and paid our costs. I sent
my friend Crosland down to see the Dons of one
of our Universities who were responsible for a
certain publication, and he sat solemnly with these
learned and reverend signors, in the cloistered seclusion of —— College, while they solemnly settled
the terms of an apology and tried to make the costs
pounds instead of guineas by promising to dismiss
their editor. From time to time, too, outsiders took
a hand at the game. It was through the tender
offices of these people that I had steady reminders
of the existence of mysterious letters which were
being held by one of them, and which were to be
produced for my destruction when this gentleman
might deem the occasion to have arisen.

CHAPTER XVI

WILDE once said to me when we were discussing poetry that there were two ways of disliking poetry—one being to dislike it, and the other to like Pope. This remark was brought forth really by Aubrey Beardsley, who was present, and who said that for him, at any rate, there was only one English poet, namely, Pope. It is highly characteristic of Wilde, who, although he insisted on his own eminence as a poet and a critic of poetry, never committed himself to what might be considered a serious theory on the subject. Piecing together the views he expressed from time to time in a casual and general way, I am convinced, indeed, that he had no theory which was in the least stable or cogent and which was not liable to be altered by the moment's whim or mood. It is certain that, while he hankered after poetic distinction and in his early manhood strove after it, his aim was not so much to produce great poetry as to turn out stuff which would provoke the critics to write about him and the witlings to talk about him. He published a volume of poems when he was twenty-six years of age, but after that he produced next to nothing poetical till he wrote the "Ballad of Reading Gaol." "The Sphinx," it is true, was published in 1894, but it had been written many years before.

In his preface to "Wilde's Selected Poems," Mr. Ross tells us that Wilde's early work was never "until recently" well received by the critics. He adds, however, that "they have survived the test of nine editions," with the "nine" in capital letters. For myself, I do not admit that the poems have been well received by criticism, even recently, for the very simple reason that there is very little in them to receive. Of course, it is unfair to apply the test of "reception" to any poetry that is worth talking about, just as it is unfair to rely on the test of editions. To take an instance in point: there is Miss Ella Wheeler Wilcox, who has been received with all manner of plaudits by all manner of reviewers and whose works have stood the test of probably ninety editions. But who in his senses is going to tell us that this estimable lady is a great poetess and to be mentioned in the same breath as—say—Mrs. Browning or Mrs. Meynell, the latter of whom, at any rate, has not achieved even so many editions as Wilde? It is plain that the only real test of

poetry is its quality, and neither its reception nor its
saleability can affect that quality. If we apply such
a test to Wilde's early poetical work, which repre-
sents the bulk of what he accomplished, we shall not
find that he shines with anything like the effulgence
that his adherents have imagined for him. Wilde
himself knew that he was not a great poet. His
cry is, continually: "I am an artist—the supreme
artist, in fact," and never: "I am a poet," or "I am
the supreme poet." He knew perfectly well that
that cock wouldn't fight. He was not even anxious
to be known as a poet in the way that some of his
contemporaries were anxious to be known. He told
me that to be dubbed "poet" was to raise up visions
of untidy hair, dirty linen, and no dinner to speak
of, and such a view of himself he abhorred. "Never
be a poet, my dear Bosie: be a gentleman, a connoisseur, an artist—what you will; but not a poet.
Let us leave being a poet to Dowson and Arthur
Symons and, if you like, Dick Le Gallienne." All
Wilde's biographers have striven manfully and—
one might say—pitifully to make a great poet out
of Oscar Wilde, and they have failed. Even Mr.
Ransome, the most zealous of the bunch, cannot
bring himself to any more flattering conclusion than
that Wilde was a sort of inspired plagiarist or imi-
tator who, in Mr. Ransome's view, improved upon

what he appropriated. Nobody who has read any poetry other than Wilde's can fail to perceive that, leaving out the "Ballad of Reading Gaol" and, up to a point, "The Sphinx," Wilde's poetical work consists of clever, and occasionally, perhaps, brilliant imitations. Wherever one turns in the three hundred pages of his published poems one finds echoes —and little else but echoes. His sonnets are, for the most part, Miltonic in their effects; the metre and method of "In Memoriam" are used in the greater number of his lyrics; and he uses the metre which Tennyson sealed to himself for all time even in "The Sphinx," which is his great set work; while in such pieces as "Charmides," "Panthea," "Humanitad" and "The Burden of Itys" he borrows the grave pipe of Matthew Arnold and what he himself called the silver-keyed flute of Keats. Haphazard, I take up the Ross-edited volume "Poems by Oscar Wilde," and I open, on page two hundred and twenty-two—"La Mer":—

> A white mist drifts across the shrouds,
> A wild moon in this wintry sky
> Gleams, like an angry lion's eye,
> Out of a mane of tawny clouds.
>
> The muffled steersman at the wheel
> Is but a shadow in the gloom:
> And in the throbbing engine-room
> Leap the long rods of polished steel.

> The shattered storm has left its trace
> Upon this huge and heaving dome,
> For the thin threads of yellow foam
> Float on the waves, like ravelled lace.

The bird is Wilde, the plumage and call are Tennyson's to a fault.

Then again, on page one hundred and thirty-six:—

> To outer senses there is peace,
> A dreamy peace on either hand;
> Deep silence in the shadowy land,
> Deep silence where the shadows cease;
>
> Save for a cry that echoes shrill
> From some lone bird disconsolate:
> A corn-crake calling to its mate,
> The answer from the misty hill.
>
> And suddenly the moon withdraws
> Her sickle from the lightening skies,
> And to her sombre cavern flies,
> Wrapped in a veil of yellow gauze.

More Tennyson, with the "In Memoriam" verse lines arbitrarily and wrongfully disposed for the deception of the innocent. I might go on quoting from Wilde in the metre *ad nauseam* and never strike so much as four lines which can be pronounced to be pure Wilde. With "The Sphinx," as a whole, I shall deal later; but I may point out here that while Wilde arranges the stanzas as though they consisted of two lines, they really consist of Tennyson's four and, for correctness' sake, should have been printed thus:—

> In a dim corner of my room
>   For longer than my fancy thinks,
>   A beautiful and silent Sphinx
> Has watched me through the shifting gloom.
>
> Inviolate and immobile,
>   She does not rise, she does not stir;
>   For silver moons are naught to her,
> And naught to her the suns that reel.

Tennyson's suns as well as Tennyson's stanza! I am not suggesting that all this is otherwise than neat and deft and skilful and pleasing, but a poet of parts, leaving out the "true poet" so beloved of Mr. Ross, should surely have a note or tone or cadence of his own, and not warble so distressingly like the "true poet" in the next street. As the Wilde faction appear to be acquainted with no poetry but "poor dear Oscar's," I will take a few passages from "In Memoriam," which, while they will be familiar to the more intelligent reader, will doubtless come in the way of an eye-opener to people like Mr. Ross. Let us repeat, to begin with, the second verse of "La Mer":—

> The muffled steersman at the wheel
> Is but a shadow in the gloom:
> And in the throbbing engine-room
> Leaps the long rods of polished steel.

This is, as we have seen, Wilde. Against it let us put Tennyson's

> I hear the noise about the keel,
>   I hear the bell struck in the night;
>   I see the cabin-window bright;
> I see the sailor at the wheel.

If ever there was an impudent and unblushing "crib," surely we have it here! I wonder what the Ransomes, Sherards, Harrises and Inglebys of this little world would say if they caught anybody else but Wilde at pretty little tricks of this kind. In Wilde such childish conveyance must be excused and even held up to admiration; in another it would be sheer theft. Then, again, take the second set of stanzas I have quoted from Wilde, about peace and silence, and compare them with the following from "In Memoriam":—

> Calm is the morn, without a sound,
>   Calm as to suit a calmer grief,
>   And only through the faded leaf
> The chestnut pattering to the ground:

> Calm and deep peace on this high wold,
>   And on these dews that drench the furze,
>   And all the silvery gossamers
> That twinkle into green and gold:

Calm and still light on yon great plain
  That sweeps with all its autumn bowers,
  And crowded farms and lessening towers,
To mingle with the bounding main:

Calm and deep peace in this wide air,
  These leaves that redden to the fall;
  And in my heart, if calm at all,
If any calm, a calm despair:

Wilde's verses are plainly a paraphrase—and a bad one to boot. It will be urged that he wrote these in his youth, and that all poets, more or less, echo one another when they are young. But when one comes to consider that out of the forty or so lyrical pieces which Wilde wrote no fewer than eighteen are in the metre of "In Memoriam," and not one of them is free from images, phrases or cadences which can easily be paralleled out of Tennyson, while the whole of "The Sphinx" is open to criticism on the same grounds, one cannot doubt that Oscar Wilde is a poet who has rather overdone the youthful imitation business; and one can scarcely be expected to break the alabaster box of critical adulation at his feet.

I have not space to enter into great detail with regard to those lyrics of Wilde which are not flatly Tennysonian. There are about twenty of them, and they include a cheap imitation of "La Belle Dame sans Merci," a flagrant copy of Hood's lines beginning "Take her up tenderly," and sundry pieces which are childishly reminiscent of Mrs. Browning, William Morris and even Jean Ingelow. Of his own initiative, Mr. Ross heads up this collection of poetical brummagem with such taking titles as "Eleutheria," "Windflowers," "Flowers of Gold," "The Fourth Movement" and "Flowers of Love." But the fact that they are wood-pulp or ceraceous replicas of other people's nosegays is of no account to the faithful and the blind.

As regards the sonnets, which may, perhaps, be said to constitute that part of Wilde's poetical work which is best worth consideration, I have only to say that while it would be tedious to compare them side by side with the sonnets of Milton and other writers, such a comparison cannot fail to convince any reasonable being that in this department again Wilde was an over-sedulous ape—so over-sedulous, in fact, that he is careful to emphasise and exaggerate the very faults and defects of his masters. On the point of technique, the importance of which cannot be too gravely insisted upon where the sonnet form is concerned, he is continuously and hopelessly at fault. His rhyme-sounds are, for the most part, of the cheapest and the most hackneyed. Of the twenty-eight sonnets which he produced, seven have rhymes to "play," "say," "day," and so forth;

rhymes to "see," "be" and "me" are common, and in even greater number; and on no fewer than twenty-one distinct occasions are we proffered such rhymes as "liberty," "anarchy," "memory," "democracy," "already," "victory," "luxury," and the like, or an average of three times in every four sonnets. And this, if you please, is the work of "the supreme artist!"

It follows without saying that while Wilde believed himself to be writing in the Italian sonnet form, he persistently finds himself unable to adhere to the difficult rules of that form. He has octaves with four rhymes in them instead of two, and he will wind up a sextet with a couplet like the veriest tyro of them all. The contents of the sonnets represent the best of Wilde's thought, being, for the most part, free from fleshliness, cynicism and perversity. Yet, when one has said this for it, one has said all. There is nowhere anything very great or very noble or very beautiful, and one never catches even a suggestion of the large accent which makes a poet. Sententiousness, grandioseness, and a laboured classicism set forward with the help of an artificial rhetoric which at times is almost comic are the upshot of Wilde's sonnets taken generally and in the lump.

There now remain the set pieces such as "A Garden of Eros," *à la* Matthew Arnold; "The New Helen," *à la* Keats; "The Burden of Itys," *à la* Matthew Arnold again; "Panthea," a blend of Matthew Arnold and Keats; and "Humanitad," more Arnold; also "The Sphinx" and the "Ballad of Reading Gaol." No lover of poetry in a high sense is likely to waste much time in the perusal of the five pieces first mentioned. It is not claimed for them by anybody that they are other than cold and super-painted failures, produced in the spirit of "Now, let me show you what I, the scholar and a connoisseur, can do," rather than by any spiritual or poetical impulsion. Only the meagrest portions of them can be admired, even by the elect; and these portions are not edifying.

As for "The Sphinx," even if we concede that the uneasy effect of its metre be dismissed from the question, we have left what is—on the face of it— a work of not always too successful virtuosity on a theme which is frankly bestial. There is an undoubted pomp and swing about some of the stanzas; there are pictures well visualised and put on the canvas with a fine eye for colour; and the element of curiousness or weirdness is well sustained; but right through the piece one is made to feel that it is not the poet but the mechanician who has come before us, and continually he creaks and whirrs, as it

were, for want of oil and control. Wilde, doubtless, set out to build a jewelled palace for his dubious
and, if you come to look at it closely, loathsome
fancy. He has succeeded only in establishing a
sort of Wardour Street receptacle for old, tarnished
and too-vividly-coloured lots. His efforts to do
things in the most dazzling and wizardly manner
are at times ludicrous, and his endeavours to get up
unthinkable passions provoke one to laughter rather
than awe. In a despairing determination to tie to
the end of the poem something on which a reasonable being might ponder, he becomes utterly in-
consequential.

False Sphinx! False Sphinx! By reedy Styx old Charon
    leaning on his oar,
Waits for my coin. Go thou before, and leave me to my
    crucifix,
Whose pallid burden, sick with pain, watches the world with
    wearied eyes,
And weeps for every soul that dies, and weeps for every soul
    in vain.

The dragging in of this bit of specious religiosity
as a *bonne bouche* after an orgy of flamboyant
passion-slaking is, doubtless, very cunning and
clever, but it has nothing to do with either great
art on the one hand or common sense on the other.
"The Sphinx" is a poem which may well have
stirred certain resorts in the neighbourhood of

Piccadilly Circus to their foundations. It is a poem for the perverse and the "curious," but its value as art or poetry is next door to negligible.

I have already said that in my view the "Ballad of Reading Gaol" is the only poem of Wilde's which is likely to endure. It is as different from his previous work as chalk is different from cheese, and to read it after perusal of "The Sphinx" or the sonnets, it might almost be the work of another hand. In point of fact, it was indeed written by a Wilde who had very little in common, whether intellectually or artistically, with the Wilde of the bulk of the poems. Up to the time of his imprisonment Oscar Wilde, poet, had encouraged, or pretended to encourage, certain very grave fallacies with regard to poetry. He asserted—largely, I think, because he knew himself to be incapable of sincerity—that poetry was, in its essence, a matter of pretence and artifice. He held that style was everything, and feeling nothing; that poetry should be removed as well from material actuality as from the actuality of the spirit, and that no great poet had ever in his greatest moments been other than insincere. He professed other odd views and used roundly to assert that he would rather have written Swinburne's "Poems and Ballads" than anything else in literature; and that Shakespeare was not, after all, a very great poet. I remember that when some idiot talked of starting an "Anti-Shakespeare Society," on the ground that "Shakespeare never wrote a line of poetry in his life," Wilde was vastly tickled by the idea, and said that Shakespeare had been much overrated. He would have it that Webster's "Duchess of Malfi" was a much better play and much better poetry than any of Shakespeare's, and, as he admired little that he did not sooner or later try to imitate, it is possible that we owe his "Duchess of Padua" to this view. In any case, up to the time of his going to prison, there can be no question that Wilde was peculiar and in a great measure heretical in his notions about what poetry should be. His opinions may or may not have altered while he was in prison. I never heard him renounce them, but after he came out he did arrive at a perception of the fact that a poet who wishes to be heard must make his appeal to the human heart as well as to the intellect, and that perversity is never by any chance poetry. And so he set about the "Ballad of Reading Gaol." Even here, however, he could not walk alone. He must have models, and his actual model was "The Dream of Eugene Aram," with "The Ancient Mariner" thrown in on technical grounds. The result, of course, far outdistances "Eugene Aram," just as in certain ultimate qualities it falls far short of "The Ancient Mariner." It is sufficient for us that in the "Ballad of Reading Gaol" we have a sustained poem of sublimated actuality and of a breadth and sweep and poignancy such as had never before been attained in this line. The emotional appeal is, on the whole, quite legitimate and, if we except a very few passages in which the old Adam Wilde crops out, the established tradition as to what is fitting and comely in a poem of this nature is not outraged or transgressed. Because of this and the general skill and deftness of its workmanship, the poem will last, and, though I cannot agree with those critics who desire to place Wilde among the Immortals, I am certainly of opinion that it is on the "Ballad of Reading Gaol" and on the "Ballad of Reading Gaol" alone that his reputation among posterity will stand.

The placing of poets and poetry in their proper relation to the mass of literature is no fool's job, and I am aware that the opinion of one age is frequently stultified by the opinion of the next. But this is not true of great work. I think it can be established that all great work has been admired and treasured from the beginning. From time to time, too, the vast quantities of mediocre and insignificant work is also admired, but in the nature of things there is no vitality about it and, despite the pæan of fools, it perishes. Much that Wilde has strung into verse will so perish. The "Ballad" may persist and save him from the oblivion which he seems to me assiduously to have courted.

CHAPTER XVII

I HAVE demonstrated in the foregoing chapter the absolute folly of Wilde's claim to supremacy as an artist. It is a claim which would never have been put forward for him if he had not put it forward for himself, but it is a claim which his adherents have constantly reiterated since his death, with nobody to gainsay them; and so vociferous and persistent have these people been that the idea of Wilde's supreme artistry has come to be accepted without question by a gaping public and to pass current as good, sound, critical coin even among the cultivated. Wilde the supreme artist in the capacity of poet does not exist and never has existed. We have now to turn to Wilde the supreme proseman. The Ross-Ransome faction are nothing if not wonderful in this regard. Their one cry, which they repeat with parrot-like iteration and to which they cling as a drowning critic might cling to critical straws, is this—Wilde's own saying: "The fact of a man being a poisoner is nothing against his prose." Now, this is such a truism that, of itself, it is not worth talking about, but it has been put up for the defence and glorification of Wilde, in and out of season. Even our great literary judge, Mr. Justice Darling, takes his cue from this remark and tells twelve English jurymen that because a man was a bad man, that is not to say that we are to refrain from reading his books, and so on. But all these people miss the real point, which is that, though the fact of a man being a poisoner is nothing against his prose, it is equally, and just as clearly, nothing for it. Without going further into the question at the moment, I shall venture to deal with Wilde's prose writings on the assumption that if they are no worse they are certainly no better through the fact of the shamefulness of his life. Wilde himself never made any great fuss about his prose writings other than the plays. He regarded—and very properly regarded—the essays in "Intentions," together with the fairy tales and his other stories (excepting, of course, "The Picture of Dorian Gray"), as so much donkey work, and pretty well on the level with his lectures, which were written for the pure purpose of getting money and with no eye to "supreme artistry." "Intentions" was first published in 1891. Three years went by before the book passed into its second edition. The first edition was published at 7s. 6d., and I believe I am right in saying that the second edition, published at 3s. 6d., was simply a "remainder" of the first in a cheaper binding. It was not till after Wilde's imprisonment and death and after the "boosters" had been at work on him for some years that we began to hear of the marvellous artistry and genius which this volume is alleged to exhibit. Wilde himself would have laughed in his sleeve if he could have been told that such preposterous claims would ever be made for his pot-boiling fleers and ironies. He knew that the "Decay of Lying," the "Critic as Artist" and the "Truth of Masks" were, in a large measure, cribbed from Whistler, and he knew that "Pen, Pencil and Poison" was the merest review article, and neither better nor worse than the average stodginess which the public of his day accepted from their somnolent monthlies. The doctrine in these papers will not bear examination. When it is good it is not Wilde's, and when it is bad it is horrid, and not necessarily Wilde's at that. It is studded with such clap-trap statements as "All art is immoral"; "Society often forgives the criminal: it never forgives the dreamer"; "There is no sin except stupidity"; "The Greeks had no art critics"; "It is difficult not to be unjust to what one loves"; "His crimes gave strong personality to his style"; "I am prepared to prove anything"; "The more we study art the less we care for nature"; "Shakespeare is too fond of going directly to life and borrowing life's natural utterance"; "Meredith is a prose Browning—and so is Browning"; "I live in terror of not being misunderstood"; "To have a capacity for a passion and not to realise it is to make oneself incomplete and limited." And so we might continue, to the complete exasperation of reason and decency. Pernicious and scurrilous stuff was always in Wilde's bosom, and if he could get it off in a sly way while pretending to discuss serious matters in a serious sense he was delighted. His doctrine was nothing more or less than a doctrine of smart negation. That he had literary skill enough and wit and scholarship enough to be entertaining nobody wishes to deny, but the cultivated people whom he entertains place no value upon his opinions. It is the middling-minded who are not entertained, and yet take him for gospel and allow such intellectuality as they may possess to be damaged and warped by his insincerities. On the whole, therefore, I say that "Intentions" will not do if we are to consider Wilde in the light of a serious and illuminating thinker.

On the ground of artistry, style and so forth the book is not by any means flawless. That Wilde had a good, easy prose style and did, at times, write accomplished prose I admit; but in this regard he stands on no better level than Mr. Frank Harris or Mr. Gilbert Chesterton.   All three of them—Wilde, Harris and Chesterton—are killed by the exuberance of their own facility.   They have the pen of the ready writer and they fall accordingly.   Moreover, Wilde is prone to the over-sugared and over-gilded passage; even though he can be as bald as the baldest and as limping as the lamest.   Of his minor defects I will say nothing, except that his split infinitives are a standing disgrace to him.

We may now pass to his stories.   I have always held that if Wilde was anything at all he was an inventor of stories.   Such social success as he ever attained was almost entirely due to this gift coupled with a remarkable delivery and a good voice.   "I have thought of a story" was an announcement for ever on his lips, and his intimates knew that five times out of six the story would be worth listening to.   When I first knew him his pet stories were of the order of the inverted fable; somewhat in the manner of the fables of Ambrose Bierce.   Two examples which have never been published I may set down here.   One of them is what Wilde called "The True Story of Androcles and the Lion."   He said that though Androcles may have been an early

Christian slave, he was also a dentist. A certain lion found himself suffering from severe toothache and consulted Androcles on the subject. The dentist advised gold filling for the back teeth and an entirely new set of teeth for the upper jaw or mandible. Later, Androcles, because he was a good Christian, was thrown to the lions or, rather, to a lion, and perceiving when the beast was let loose upon him that here was an old friend, approached him with joy, feeling sure that the lion would not hurt him inasmuch as he had made no charge for the gold filling and the upper set of teeth. But the King of Beasts had other views and promptly tore Androcles to pieces, and chewed him up with the very teeth which had been so kindly and generously supplied to him.

And the other story was called "Presence of Mind." "In a theatre in America," said Wilde, "there was a young flute-player who was gifted with an extraordinary presence of mind. One evening some of the scenery caught fire and, as the smoke and flames began to rush into the building, the audience prepared to flee. Whereupon, with singular presence of mind, the young flute-player jumped out of his seat and, holding up a lily-white hand, cried in stentorian tones: 'There is no danger!' In consequence of these words the audience kept their seats and every single soul of them was burnt to death. Thus we may see," added Wilde, "how useful a thing presence of mind really is."

Of course, he had other stories in different veins, and I believe that all the tales in "The Happy Prince" and "The House of Pomegranates," as well as in the volume which contains "Lord Arthur Saville's Crime," were told by Wilde over and over again before they were written; just as he told the tale of "La Sainte Courtisane" and the plots of his plays before they were written. "The Happy Prince" and "The House of Pomegranates" are not without their merits as fairy tales in the manner of Hans Andersen, but Wilde could not be content with the simplicities of his model, and some of the stories are marred by the obliquities of the cynic and the perverse mind.

"Lord Arthur Saville's Crime" and the stories printed with it may be said to represent Wilde's attempt to come up with Robert Louis Stevenson on the plane of the New Arabian Nights. For my own part, I do not think that any of them quite "comes off." Wilde's friends have been at great pains to dilate on their "exquisite charm," their "mordant humour," and so forth; but they have always seemed to me to be fairly feeble. "Lord

Arthur Saville's Crime" itself is so over-fantastical that it becomes farcical. "The Canterville Ghost," which Wilde describes as a hylo-idealistic romance, is a feeble but unblushing imitation of a now forgotten story called "Cecilia de Noel," by Lane Falconer. "The Sphinx, Without a Secret," is a very stale and flat disappointment; and "The Model Millionaire" is exactly the kind of story for which *Tit-Bits* or *Answers* gives a guinea prize every week. I should not like the reader to imagine that I am dismissing these things airily or pooh-poohing them for the mere sake of doing it. I have lately read them with care, and I marvel that anybody can pretend that there is a great or dazzling merit about them.

I believe that at the bottom of his heart Wilde felt that his true genius had found expression in his plays. Being the man he was, he could not refrain from praising his own poetry, his own essays and stories, and professing that they were very fine things indeed; but when he talked of himself as a supreme artist, it was the plays that he always had looming in his mind. For his poetry he had never received any of the critical rewards which would have so delighted him. He was never hailed poet by the poets contemporary with him; never admitted to that higher hierarchy to which

Tennyson, Swinburne, Arnold, Browning and, if you like, even Rossetti, felt and knew themselves to belong. But his general prose and some of his essays (paid for lavishly by Frank Harris when he was editing *The Fortnightly*) made a nine days' sensation, but they brought him no real credit or reputation; neither did the story books. It was with *Lady Windermere's Fan* that he first got home, as it were; with results which, in the way of finance and applause, were entirely beyond his wildest dreams or expectation. *Lady Windermere's Fan* was a success, as successes went in those days, and it was followed by other successes, culminating in *The Importance of being Earnest*, which brought Wilde more money and more appreciation than any of them. Because the plays were a success and London went to see them, Wilde allowed himself to think that they must be important as literature and that he was a great dramatist.

Sir Arthur Pinero will probably not consider himself too flattered when I mention that Wilde had the greatest possible admiration for his work, and told me that from Pinero and Dumas Fils he had learnt all he knew of stagecraft and that he considered *The Magistrate* to be the best of all modern comedies. It is certain that for the plays, as for everything else he did, Wilde had to model himself on somebody, and Sir Arthur is fortunate or unfortunate in having been the man. One has only to compare the constructive methods of the two to recognise this. The only difference between them is that Sir Arthur Pinero maintains an illusion of strict sanity among his characters, whereas Wilde is not always to be depended upon in this regard. Besides which, there is the further difference that, while Pinero conforms to the established code of morals and makes his good people good and his bad people bad, Wilde has a tendency to hold up bad people for good people, and drops out really good people altogether. I am going to say this much and no more about the plays as a body: namely, that they put Wilde into a secondary position with regard to Pinero and Mr. Sydney Grundy.

His plays are not literary or intellectual plays, but just the conventional things which were stirring in London during Wilde's period, with the Wilde paradox, irony, flippancy and insincerity thrown in. I am no frantic believer in the supreme gifts of Mr. George Bernard Shaw, and I have never been able to get up any great enthusiasm for the sentimentalities of Sir J. M. Barrie; but it is quite certain that both these gentlemen have beaten Wilde as exponents of a drama which is supposed to be concerned with art and literature rather than with the stage and the box-office.

Wilde will not last as a dramatist, whether behind the footlights or in the closet. His plays have been revived occasionally, and the glitter has been found in a great measure to have died out of them; while as plays for reading they would not be read at all if they bore any other name but Wilde's. I will ask any unbiassed person to peruse *Lady Windermere's Fan* or, if you like, *An Ideal Husband* and *The Importance of being Earnest,* and tell me if here is great work. I do not wish to load these pages with quotations from books which are readily obtainable; but if I were so disposed I could set forth twaddling and mock-heroic dialogue and feeble humour from Wilde's plays by the yard. There are passages in all the plays which might have been written by a sentimental schoolgirl rather than by an artist, or by a giggling actor rather than a wit. I shall not say that the plays failed of their purpose, which, however, could have been at best only a temporary purpose. A man who boasted of the intellectual superiorities of which Wilde boasted, demeaned himself when he wrote them, and still more hopelessly demeaned himself when he pretended to take the popular applause which followed for honest fame. I was constantly with him, as I have shown,. when he wrote the most successful of them. In a careless way I aided and abetted him in their production, but it never entered my mind that they were either fine drama or fine literature. And whatever Wilde himself might have thought about them, he certainly would not have contended that they were wonderful works or genius before me. I do not wish to suggest that a man of genius is not entitled to condescend to the demands of the popular stage in certain circumstances, such as need of money or a desire to show that genius can do common things quite as capably as common people; and it is therefore that I do not blame Wilde for writing the prose plays. But it is obviously illogical and idiotic of him to turn round and profess that because he could tickle the popular fancy of his period, the work with which he did it is as fine and as worthy as anything in dramatic literature. Nobody knew better than he how false and foolish and how subversive of reason such an assumption must be. Wilde's "boomsters" have gone further in this stupid business than even Wilde himself would have gone. If we are to believe what they write, Wilde is the greatest dramatist since Shakespeare, and beats Goldsmith, Congreve, Sheridan and all the rest of them into a cocked hat. The cold truth is that he never succeeded in rivalling Sir Arthur Pinero or Mr. Jones, and that he has been out-distanced by his own pupil, Mr. George Bernard Shaw.

CHAPTER XVIII

THERE is a critical shibboleth to the effect that no man can rightly judge his contemporaries. The true inwardness of this very comforting idea lies in its extreme utility where persons of mediocre intellect are concerned. Persons who write feeble poetry and silly plays, not to mention offensive fiction, always pretend to put their hopes in posterity. My contention is that posterity is not likely to be much more imbecile than the contemporary world, and that the foolish hopes of vain and incompetent people are consequently ill-founded. A feeble poem is not to be strengthened by the mere process of time any more than a piece of strong work is likely to be weakened or degraded. It is singular to note, too, that people seldom appeal to posterity when they are being applauded. For a man with bouquets in his hand and the laurel on his brow posterity does not exist. On the other hand, for all of us, whoever we may be, posterity has its use, and, though I do not think that

226

these uses are important to us, they nevertheless exist. By way, therefore, of a sporting offer, as it were, I shall reach a hand through time and ask posterity to do me a favour, which is this: when I have been dead fifty years let some critic of parts put on one side Wilde's published work, the present work and my own poems and verses; and let him put on the other side all the biographies of Wilde he can lay his hand on, together with the parts of "De Profundis" which are now lying in the British Museum; and when he has examined carefully and critically these two bundles of material, let him say without fear or favour who has drawn the true picture—Lord Alfred Douglas or Messrs. Ross, Ransome, Sherard and Harris.

I shall sink or swim on some such decision, and I am content. At the present moment it is to the interest of everybody directly concerned that the Wilde myth should continue to exist. It is excellent for Wilde's publishers, excellent for the printing, paper and bookbinding trades, and excellent for those critics and editors who are best known by their labours in connection with Wilde. For them it is merely a matter of trade, and innocent enough. It is also excellent for those depraved persons who take Wilde as their moral guide and who profess to believe—and, possibly, do believe—that the viciousness for which Wilde suffered imprisonment is a species of superior virtue; and it is also excellent for that vast multitude of persons who, while they may have no particular sympathy with Wilde's depravities, are, nevertheless, of oblique mind and cynically immoral intellect. In the aggregate these people are very strong, much stronger than the easygoing, uncorrupted masses of humanity imagine. They are so strong in England and so numerous that it is profitable to flood the country with Wilde's works at a shilling. They are so strong in the press that it is next door to impossible to find a critical review or newspaper wherein Wilde's name is not mentioned, from time to time, with bated breath and whispered humbleness. They are so strong socially that the Wilde evangelists are welcomed in the highest political and social circles. And they are so insidious that they have succeeded in upsetting the usually calm judgment of the Bench and the Bar. We have seen Mr. F. E. Smith, K.C., weeping crocodile tears over Wilde's memory and expressing the hope that his sins were forgotten and that his genius might be left to blaze brilliantly in all men's sight without so much as a rude air to disturb it.

There are two interests, however, which these bands of champions habitually ignore. One is the

KINMOUNT HOUSE, ANNAN, THE SEAT OF THE LATE MARQUIS OF QUEENSBERRY, WHERE LORD ALFRED DOUGLAS'S CHILDHOOD WAS PASSED

interest of letters and the other is the interest of the public morals. It is not in the interest of letters that any writer, however capable, should be given honour and adulation beyond his merits. When Wilde is set up for the supreme artist all other artists in all time are degraded thereby; when Wilde is set up for a poet of the first order, all other poets suffer damage by comparison; and when Wilde is set up for a moralist, there is just a lunatic, anarchist end of morals. The question of the public interest is largely bound up in these things. But outside of them there are ever graver matters. I maintain that even if we dismiss Wilde's private shamefulness from the account, he is still to be condemned by reason of the nature and intention of his writings.

As I shall show in the chapter on "Dorian Gray," Wilde himself admitted that "Dorian Gray" was a poisonous book. In its own way "The Sphinx" is just as poisonous, and so are many passages in the essays which go to make up "Intentions." In the plays we find him continually flying in the face of the rules of conduct which make life possible and keep it sweet. He preaches always (flatly or by innuendo) that vice is at least more interesting than virtue; that insincerity is better and more to be desired than truth; that cynical carelessness and indifference are more comely than kind feeling and altruism; and that the whole end and aim of life is to eat delicately, sleep softly and be as wicked and depraved as you like, provided that you are wicked and depraved in a graceful manner. I find myself utterly incapable of acquiescing in such a scandalous view of the reasons and purposes of human existence, and I say my say accordingly. It would have been easier and more profitable for me to have made a book about Wilde which would not have appeared harsh or severe or in any way offensive to the factions which ring him round. The breaking up of other people's gods, even though they happen to be gods of clay, is not a job for a man of a pacific turn of mind. Wilde knew that some day a true biographical and critical account of himself would have to be written and, doubtless, on the principle of getting one's blow in first, he put it on record that it is always Judas who is the biographer. The late lamented Charles Peace was of the same opinion, and so, doubtless, were many other unpleasant and somewhat exploded persons, accounts of whose lives have still to be written. It is conceivable that there are circumstances in which honest biography is of slight consequence. In point of fact, all biography that matters is largely a sort of exegesis and commentary on the life work of its subject. The biographies of persons who have done nothing are, in the nature of things, unprofitable. Wilde made a stir in the world, and his drum-beaters and fuglemen have made an even greater stir on his behalf. It is right and proper that while the noise is still in the air we should endeavour to discover its real meaning and to get sight of the instruments by which it is produced.

CHAPTER XIX

I HAVE already shown that it was not until the Ransome trial was well on the way that I had any idea of the existence of the unpublished parts of "De Profundis" or that the whole manuscript had originally been couched in the form of a letter to me. As soon as I heard rumours of these facts I communicated with Mr. Robert Ross, and was informed definitely of them by Messrs. Lewis and Lewis, who, in their letter to me, asserted that "I must have known" of the existence of the manuscript and that my name was omitted from the published parts out of "consideration for my feelings." It is perfectly obvious that there is nothing in the published parts of "De Profundis" to which I could take exception, nor should I have been in the least degree injured if Mr. Ross had let it be known that the published parts were addressed to me instead of leaving it to be inferred that they had been addressed to him. It is true that when I had a conversation with him prior to the publication of the book, Ross told me that there were certain references in it which I might not have liked, but he also told me that these had been expunged, and I understood that the book was really a letter addressed to himself. This is as far as my information went up to the time of the action.

Before the trial I obtained, by order of the Court, discovery of the unpublished part of "De Profundis." I handed the document to Mr. T. W. H. Crosland, who, after perusing it, insisted on reading it to me from the first word to the last. I gave him answers then and there on every point he chose to raise, and I don't mind admitting that his examination of me was a good deal closer and a good deal keener than that of Mr. Campbell, K.C., who cross-examined me on behalf of Ransome.

It was not until we got into Court that we knew that Mr. Ross had been so kind as to hand over the unpublished parts of the "De Profundis" MS. to the authorities of the British Museum as a present to the nation with the condition that they were to remain under seal till 1960, and that the British Museum authorities had been gracious enough to accept the gift. It is not for me to profess to know upon what principle the British Museum accepts gifts of secret documents. One takes it that somebody at the British Museum must have taken the trouble to read the MS. before it was accepted and sealed up, and that unless the person who perused it was a sheer idiot he must have perceived that it contained much scurrilous and libellous matter not only concerning myself, but concerning the Dowager Marchioness of Queensberry and other members of my family. Yet the MS. was accepted and is now in possession and control of the officials at the British Museum. With these facts before us we are brought face to face with an entirely new and unprecedented range of possibilities. I flatter myself that when I die any lengthy MS. of mine which I might care to write would have some slight value for persons concerned in the collection of holographs and similar material for museums. It is open to me, therefore, to sit down and write a villainous attack upon any eminent person with whom I may chance to be acquainted and to arrange that my executor shall present it to the British Museum to be treasured for the nation and put to such uses as the British Museum may at any time deem to be fitting. How many manuscripts of this nature may already be lurking on the British Museum's shelves the wise authorities alone know. Fifty years hence we may wake up to a due knowledge of the "real" characters of most of our most noted public men, written by other eminent public men who have had real or imaginary grievances against them. It may well be that we shall have the pleasure of reading Mr. Lloyd George's inside opinions of Lord Reading and his brethren, written in Mr. Lloyd George's own hand at the National Liberal Club in moments of irritation or depression after the Marconi affair. Possibly Mr. Keir Hardie may have consigned to the same safe and honourable keeping some of his extraordinary opinions about certain dukes and certain judges; and to come into other fields, Mr. Clement K. Shorter may have lodged his private and innermost view of the character and habits of Sir William Robertson Nicoll, Mr. Thomas Hardy, Miss Marie Corelli, and heaven and the British Museum alone know whom else besides. And what a chance is herein opened up for Mr. Frank Harris! He has known and apparently loved Carlyle, Huxley, Meredith, Matthew Arnold and Oscar Wilde, not to mention Lord Randolph Churchill, Mr. Asquith, Mr. Ben Tillet and other notabilities. He has nothing to do but to write what he likes about them and present the result to the British Museum, for opening and publication in that *annus mirabilis* 1960.

Of course, it is ridiculous to suppose that any of the persons I have mentioned possess spleen and impudence enough to degrade themselves by doing anything of the kind. But the fact remains that the British Museum authorities are sitting at the receipt of custom, with open and itching palms, and that in Wilde's case they have received, and, not only so, but have refused to disgorge when they were caught at it.

I quite admit that, having once accepted on behalf of the nation a relic of any kind, the British Museum is bound to be cautious about parting with it again. This, doubtless, is the refuge behind which the authorities take their stand; but the real point is whether they were ever justified in accepting it at all, and whether, in any case, it was in the public interest that such a manuscript should be accepted. In law, the paper on which any letter is written belongs to the person to whom it is addressed. The "De Profundis" manuscript is addressed to me, on the face of it, and I hold that I have a moral if not a legal right to its possession. But leaving this aspect of the question on one side, the British Museum authorities will surely not contend that it is to the interest of anybody in the world, other than those persons who delight in scandal, backbiting and malice, that such a manuscript should be preserved. What possible motive that is worthy can be offered as an excuse by these people? Argue as they will, they must perceive that the manuscript is one which in no conceivable circumstances can be considered to reflect anything but discredit on its author. When it is published— and it will be out of copyright one day—Oscar Wilde is finished. No reputation, however securely founded, can hope to survive the moral *débâcle* which this manuscript demonstrates to have taken place in the mind of Oscar Wilde. It is said that there must be honour even among thieves. A man may do despicable things and still retain a share of the respect of his fellow-men. Murderers have gone to their doom and have yet compelled some sort of respect from the world in the manner of their doing it. As the published reports of the Ransome trial show, Wilde has whined and shuffled and protested and wept and tried to shift his responsibilities to innocent shoulders; and the British Museum is to make a public treasure of the record of his infamy and keep it for him until such time as it may be published without unpleasant legal consequences.

For myself I do not care tuppence about the contents of this manuscript. I was anxious that it should be read out word for word in Court at the Ransome trial. If this had been done, and the counsel for the defence had dared to cross-examine me on it in detail, I should have won my

case. On the insistence of my counsel a pretence
was made of reading it, but not twenty pages had
been got through before Mr. Justice Darling intervened, and the reading of the MS. as a whole was
discontinued. Thereafter only such portions were
read as were supposed to be greatly to my detriment. Although these passages were read, I was
never so much as asked, either by judge or counsel,
to say if there was any truth in them. Wilde had
written them in mad rage when he was caged up in
a squalid gaol, a disgraced and whimpering convict,
and, of course, they must be true! The judge himself pointed out that prisoners are apt to slander
and unreason, but he did not tell the jury that they
must take no notice of what had been read. Oscar
Wilde had written it, Oscar Wilde was a man of
genius, and they must form their own conclusions.
The veriest tyro in law will tell you that such a document as this is no evidence at all and ought not to
have been admitted. Yet it was admitted and parts
selected by the defence were allowed to go to the
jury. I think that common sense and common justice demanded that we should have had all or none.
If the British Museum authorities did not fully
appreciate the nature of the manuscript at the time
of its acceptance they have had every opportunity
of making themselves conversant with its meaning

and intention through what took place at the trial. They must surely have recognised that it is capable of being put—and, indeed, has been put—to the basest and most cowardly uses, and that it is, in essence, of absolutely no other use. For all that, it is still preserved, as though it were a literary gem of the first water instead of something which mankind at large would be quite willing to let die. I am in no position to fight the British Museum for the possession of this abominable curiosity. If it had come into my hands at any time prior to the Ransome trial it would have been simply thrown on the fire, not because I am afraid of it or because any of my family are afraid of it, but because, when all is said, I should have had too much respect for Wilde's memory and too much regard for letters ever to consent to its publication. But it has never been in my hands, and it is now no longer possible for it to be kept secretly. Responsible persons at the British Museum may well be left to their own reflections upon the wisdoms of preserving this mummified libel.

CHAPTER XX

I AM not going to trouble the reader with an account of the "Life and Works" of Mr. Arthur Ransome, one of whose claims to fame lies in the fact that he was a defendant in the Ransome trial. His critical study of Oscar Wilde is a lumbering, apologetic performance dedicated to Robert Ross and with an evident regard for the opinions of Ross even where criticism is concerned. The passages in it which I held to be libellous upon myself have been expunged, and, according to Ransome, this was done with a view to sparing my feelings. The edition current among the public, however, is not published by the original publishing house, but by another firm, and both this firm and Mr. Ransome will, doubtless, be startled to hear that if they had ventured to insert the passages of which I complained in the edition for which they are responsible I should have immediately served writs for libel upon them and taken my chances of another "evisceration" in the witness-box. Possibly Mr.

Ransome had no inkling of this when he put his wonderfully magnanimous note to the new edition, but his publishers are wise people.

Ransome's "Critical Study," at a shilling, has been planted on Smith's stalls and at all the shilling bookselling booths throughout the country, ever since the trial, with the name "Oscar Wilde" printed large on the dust cover, and the name of "Ransome" not quite so large. I am going to take the edition as it stands, because the original edition was withdrawn by the publishers and can only have had a very limited circulation. It deals with the facts of Wilde's life in the briefest way, and is devoted mainly to a pretentious discussion of Wilde's writings. I may best sum up its critical announcements by saying that they are all of them what Ross would have liked them to be. Beginning with the poems, Ransome assures us that "Ravenna" is an admirable prize poem. He tells us that Wilde's early poems are "rich in imitations" and full of "variations of other men's music," adding that they are variations to which the personality of the virtuoso has given "a certain uniformity." "Certain" is good, in view of the fact that these poems are most distinctly not uniform in any single quality which appertains to poetry. Of Wilde's apings of Milton he says: "Some of those exercises, which are among the most

interesting he wrote, suggest the new view of the
morale of imitation"; and he goes on to tell us that
"Wilde made himself, as it were, the representative
poet of his period. People who had heard of Rossetti
and Swinburne, but never read them, were able to
recover their self-respect by purchasing Wilde."
Was ever such arrant nonsense put before a con-
fiding public, even at a shilling? Mr. Ransome was
in swaddling clothes when Wilde's early volume
was going through its five editions, otherwise he
would know that for one person who "recovered
his self-respect" by purchasing Wilde there were
fifty persons who were purchasing and reading
Swinburne and Rossetti without worrying about
their self-respect at all.

Mr. Ransome is full of admiration for the early
poems as a body. He cannot deny that "the young
man's verse was grossly derivative," or that Milton,
Dante, Marlowe, Keats, Browning and others "make
up a goodly list of sufferers by this light-hearted
corsair's piracies," but he asks the reader to believe
that Wilde's plagiarism was a really pretty gift and
all to the advantage of letters, and that the poems
are to be valued as the early work of a great man
and, for that matter, a great poet. I should have
wished that Mr. Ransome might have given us a
more explicit condemnation of the moral aspect of

"The Sphinx." His final remark is that "it is as if a man were finding solace for his feverish hands in the touch of cool, hard stones, and at the same time stimulating his fever by the sexual excitement of contrast between the over-sensitive and the utterly insensible"—whatever this may mean.

On the prose Mr. Ransome spreads his butter very thick and, by way of apology and blessing for "Dorian Gray," he has the following specious paragraphs: "Perhaps the reason why it was so loudly accused of immorality was that in the popular mind luxury and sin are closely allied, and the unpardonable mannerism that made him preach in a parable against the one, did not hide his whole-hearted delight in describing the other." . . . " 'Dorian Gray,' for all its faults, is such a book. It is unbalanced; and that is a fault. It is a mosaic, hurriedly made by a man who reached out in all directions and took and used in his work whatever scrap of jasper or porphyry or broken flint was put into his hand; and that is not a virtue. But in it there is an individual essence, a private perfume, a colour whose secret has been lost. There are moods whose consciousness that essence, perfume, colour is needed to intensify."

And all this—mind you—of a book which Wilde himself called "poisonous," and which Mr. Ransome's own publishers, Messrs. Methuen, declined to include at any price in their various editions of Wilde's works. There is a great deal to pretty much the same effect about "Intentions" and the plays. Everything that Wilde has done is wonderful from the Ransome point of view, and his literary faults and failings are beautifully explained away or made the occasion for the handing up of bouquets, until we come right down to the appended somewhat mild reproof: "In 1889, before the maleficent flood of gold was poured upon him, he had become accustomed to indulge the vice that, openly alluded to in the days and verses of 'Catullus,' is generally abhorred and hidden in our own."

I have previously shown that Ransome goes out of his way in another place to indicate that Wilde's best work was done during the period when he was "an habitual devotee" to the vice in question, and he is not content even with this subtle hint, but goes on to suggest that Wilde's knowledge of his own infamy may have induced in him "a heightened ardour of production." I am aware that the impropriety of this sort of criticism can be readily explained away on the ground that it is honest or scientific; but the fact remains that such criticism must convey some vague suggestion that the literary result—in Wilde's case, at least—was an excuse for the vice. Such an impression should not be derivable from what professes to be a "critical study" of literary work.

It is the custom of all persons who wish to defend dubious or immoral publications, such as I judge some of Wilde's works to be, to assert that the same thing is done in France—which country they assert to be the Mother of all the Arts—and that nobody complains and no harm has accrued. If this were true of the French or any other people I do not know that it would be good argument; but, as a matter of fact, it is not true. Frenchmen have undoubtedly been the greatest sinners in the composition of undesirable books, and that they are beginning to reap what they have sown is quite evident from the condition of French public morals to-day. France admits that the greatest of her social problems at the moment lies in the utterly vicious and decadent tendencies of French youth, particularly of the lower and middle classes. But Frenchmen are beginning to perceive that just as the *apache* and the adolescent criminal are the direct outcome of the neglect of religious and moral teaching in the French national schools, so the unsavoury intellectual art-mongers and Wilde-worshippers who are so thick upon the ground in middle-class French society owe themselves, in the main, to the pernicious literature upon which the French law places no check. It may be useful to remember here that even in that great and glorious centre of artistic freedom—Paris—the authorities declined to allow the proposed monument to be erected over Wilde's grave in *Père la Chaise* until certain modifications had been made in the work. It was a bitter blow to some of the Wilde faction, but the authorities of Paris were inexorable, and those responsible for the monument learned a lesson that they could not do as they liked, even in France. I do not say that Mr. Ransome has anything to do with this, but I do say that anybody who, by so much as a word or a phrase, minimises Wilde's vices or vicious writing in the name of Art is not sufficiently alive to the danger of one of the most scandalous movements that has ever excited and betrayed mankind.

MONUMENT ERECTED OVER OSCAR WILDE'S GRAVE,
PÈRE LA CHAISE, PARIS

CHAPTER XXI

MY ACTIONS FOR LIBEL

THE number of writs which I have had from time to time to issue over the Wilde affair is past my count. If I had invoked the law on every occasion upon which I have been libelled over it, I suppose that the fees for writs alone would have run into hundreds of pounds. For some years I allowed people to say whatever they might choose to say about me without lifting a finger against them. I believed in Wilde, who was my friend: I believed in his genius and I had an exaggerated opinion about the value of some of his writings. It seemed to me that time would set me right; and it seemed to me important, both for Wilde's sake and the sake of letters, that I should avoid, so far as was possible, stirring up the mud which I knew lay at the bottom of his life. By the time Wilde came out of prison I formed a sort of habit of taking no notice whatever of either his or my detractors. After his death I let everybody who had known him rush into print about him without offering the slightest con-

tribution to the discussion.   Sherard produced two
books purporting to be biographies of Wilde. Other
books on Wilde have been written by various hands;
Mr. Ingleby has written a life, and I believe biographies have been published in America.   I can
honestly say, however, that I have not troubled
even to read any of these works.   Though I have
quoted from Sherard in the present volume, I have
not read either of his books through.   Ingleby's
book I have glanced at and Ransome's "Critical
Study" I read through for the first time in July of
last year.   My opinions as to the importance of
Wilde's writings began to change as my reading
extended and my mind took hold of serious things.
A man's critical judgment is not at its best at
twenty-eight, especially in regard to the artistic
productions of his intimates.   Even when we were
together I had told Wilde over and over again that
he overrated himself and that he was not by any
means the great man he believed himself to be.   To
give him his due, he agreed with me.   Nevertheless,
after his death I held his memory as a friend and,
if you like, even as a literary figure, in such regard
that I never so much as dreamed of saying or writing anything which would be likely to injure him.
We had had our differences.   I knew that he had
written me one angry letter in prison and I knew that

for reasons of their own his intimates hated me; but he had apologised to me for his anger and admitted that it was unrighteous and ill-founded. I did everything that a man could do to succour and help him and make life possible for him after he left prison; and I was unremitting in kindness to him right down to the time of his death. He, for his part, seemed to be most kindly and affectionately disposed towards me and, for aught I knew to the contrary, would gladly have done for me what I gladly did for him if our positions had been reversed.

This thing is certain: that, during the whole of our close intimacy in Naples and Paris, subsequent to his downfall, he never once said or even hinted to me that he had anything to blame me for, or that, whether as regards finance or any other matters, I had treated him otherwise than generously and as one friend should treat another. He was a clever man and, in his way, a singularly astute man, but I never imagined that he was either clever or astute enough to keep up a show of affectionate friendship for a man whom he hated during the years that elapsed between his leaving Berneval and his death. At the last he drank a great deal more than was good for him, and when alcohol began to have a power over him and make him drunk, the wine was

in and the wit was out in Oscar Wilde's case just
as in any other man's.   If he had cherished resent-
ments against me and had succeeded in hiding them
when he was sober, I should have thought he would
have given me an inkling of them when he was
drunk, but he never did.   Yet all the time the manuscript of "De Profundis" was in existence, and Mr.
Ross held his instructions to publish it.

Now, when I found in a book—which was obviously intended to be the apotheosis of Wilde, but
was dedicated to Ross, and which claimed to put
forth the major facts of Wilde's life on the authority of Ross as to biographical details—statements
to the effect that I had been in some way responsible
for his public obloquy, and that I basely deserted
him when his money was spent, I cannot see that
there was any possible course open to me but to have
the matter threshed out in a court of law.   I accordingly issued writs upon the whole of the parties
who were legally concerned: that is to say, on the
author, the publisher, the printers, and a representative firm of distributors.   The printers apologised
and the publisher withdrew the book from circulation, and they were allowed to drop out of the action.
The "Times Book Club" put in a defence on technical grounds, and Ransome, for his part, put in a
plea of justification.   That plea could never have

been framed without the assistance and co-operation of Ross. I knew perfectly well what it would, in all probability, contain before ever I saw it. It was never really put to the jury. Recourse was had to other measures. Ross was in possession of a few old letters of mine; the British Museum had the unpublished parts of "De Profundis"; *Truth* had the letters which I had addressed to Labouchere, and Messrs. Russell—a firm of solicitors of which the Honourable Charles Russell is the principal—produced—I presume under subpœna—the idiot letter from Wilde to myself which my father produced at Wilde's trial at the Old Bailey. Of my letters to Wilde, Ross and Labouchere there is, since they were not in the defendants' possession, no mention whatever in the defendants' affidavit of documents, and consequently I had no warning of them.

Of the "De Profundis" manuscript I was given due notice and, of course, I knew that Wilde's own letter—which is a letter which reflects discredit on Wilde rather than on anybody else—would be sure to turn up. So that my letters to Wilde and Ross and the letters to *Truth*—the former sixteen years old and the latter eighteen or twenty years old—were sprung on me as I stood in the witness-box. They proved absolutely nothing, but it was

natural that they should make prejudice; and I complain, not that they were produced, but that they
were produced without my being given an opportunity of perusing them and calling to mind the
circumstances in which they were written. I said
in the witness-box what I sincerely felt and feel—
namely: that I am ashamed of having written them;
but I will say here and now what I tried to say then,
which is that the other side ought to be much more
ashamed of having produced them. What the defence really did in effect was to say: "If you didn't
ruin Wilde and desert him because he had no more
money to spend on you, you did something else
which justifies us in saying anything we like about
you." In point of fact, this is always what happens
where actions for libel are concerned. You libel a
man in a most cruel and vicious way, and if he takes
an action against you you go to court and libel him
still further. Mr. Ransome got his verdict and,
though I would have appealed against it if I had
possessed the means, he is fully entitled to it in law.
He is entitled to go on saying that I ruined Wilde,
or that I lived on Wilde, till he is black in the face
if he can get anybody to print and stand the racket
of it. But who will believe him? Even with the
jury's verdict to give it sanction, the thing is too
preposterous for words. The Ransome affair had

made no particular difference to me; but what has it done for Wilde? Here were these people with two short paragraphs which had nothing to do with and could not possibly help their book in the least. When I started my action against them I did not ask for damages and should have been content with a withdrawal of the paragraphs, and, in the long run, they have had to be withdrawn. If this had been done before the trial I should never have known of the existence of the unpublished parts of "De Profundis" and the public would never have known of them till 1960. The present book would not have been written and the Wilde myth would have gone merrily on its way rejoicing, until it was exploded by process of time. So that clearly Wilde profits nothing, but, on the whole, loses disastrously and perhaps prematurely, and his tumble has been brought about by the very persons who profess to be his most devoted and zealous friends. Knowing what they must have known, and particularly knowing that I had not asked for damages, they would have taken good care that no action took place if they had sufficiently valued Wilde. They are fifteen hundred pounds out of pocket, and the radiant picture of Oscar Wilde, which they had been at pains to limn, can be radiant no more. Even Mr. Justice Darling and Mr. F. E. Smith cannot save it in its pristine beauty. The former was kind enough to explain to a crowded court that Lord Alfred Douglas "might" have achieved some success in letters if he had put his talents to assiduous use, while the latter said that Lord Alfred Douglas had, in some way which was not explained, outraged every tradition of his class. Mr. Justice Darling forgot that I am still the possessor of a pen far more able than his own, and Mr. F. E. Smith forgot that, unlike himself, I belong to a class which takes no stock in cant and is not to be put down by windy rhetoric; a class, too, which does not look to Mr. Horatio Bottomley for a push into prominence.

CHAPTER XXII

WILDE had written and published "The Picture of Dorian Gray" two years before I knew him. At the time of its appearance in *Lippincott's Magazine* I was an undergraduate at Oxford and, so far as I know, neither Wilde nor myself had ever set eyes on one another. I mention this because it has been pretended that Wilde took me for the model for one of his beastly characters. Dates are pretty stubborn things, however, and there can be no doubt whatever that "The Picture of Dorian Gray" was published in 1890. Not only so, but, by the time I came to know Wilde, the hubbub which the story had first created had altogether died away; and as I did not read the book with any sort of care or critical intention till years afterwards, it never entered into my mind that it expressed the peculiar views of life which it is said to illustrate. Wilde talked about the book sometimes as a highly moral work which had been hopelessly misunderstood by the critics,

and he gave me a copy of it in which, as was his
custom, he inscribed his name; and I did not read
the book again until the time of my father's action
against Wilde.   Even then I did not read it closely
or with any grave attention.   I took it for granted
for what Wilde says it was—namely: a work of
art with an excellent moral; and I do not wish to
say now that it is not a work of art or that it does
not point a very splendid moral for morally disposed
people.   It has been reviewed as such in more than
one important religious paper.   At the time when
I was editing *The Academy* I blamed Messrs. Methuen for not having the pluck to include the book in
their editions of Wilde's works.   It seems to me
preposterous that if a book can be sold openly at
any English bookshop it should be refused inclusion
among the author's works by his own publishers.
Since I made my protest on this matter, however,
the whole question of Wilde and his books has
undergone a marked and, to my mind, a most dangerous change.   I quite anticipated that the day
would arrive when Wilde's disgrace might, in a
sense, be dissociated from his writings.   I looked
to time and common sense to winnow out what was
good in those writings and reject what was noxious
or deleterious.   It never occurred to me that I
should live to see Wilde used in the way in which

he has been used, and is being used, to the endangerment of letters and morals. We are now face to face with this fact—namely: that there exists in England as well as in France, Germany and Russia, a distinct and recognisable Wilde cult, which has as its creed that Wilde was one of the greatest geniuses that ever lived. To this large following, which accepts Wilde's vices as a sign of genius, "The Picture of Dorian Gray" has proved to be a powerful weapon. It is a book after their own heart, and its wit and the moral which it points —or does not point, according as one may take it— enable these people to employ it in subtle and devious ways. I cannot help believing that Wilde must have intended "Dorian Gray" as a fleer at morality. In effect he may be said to have laid himself out to write a sermon the interest of which should really depend on obscenities. He puts before us one of the vilest of human creatures, and, without particularising as to the nature of his vileness, brings him to an infamous and therefore poetically just end; but the danger of the thing lies in that, while nine people out of ten could not have told you at the time of the publication of the book wherein the peculiar sin of "Dorian Gray" lay, quite ninety people out of a hundred can now tell you. What was laughed at for affectation in 1891 assumed a sinister and altogether an abominable aspect as the years went on and the true effect and intention of Wilde's work began to make itself apparent. I am not going into details, but everybody knows what I mean.

It may be interesting if I print in this place portions of a review of the story which appeared in the *St. James' Gazette* for June 24th, 1890. "Time was (it was in the '70's) when we talked about Mr. Oscar Wilde; time came (it was in the '80's) when he tried to write poetry and, more adventurous, we tried to read it; time is when we had forgotten him—or only remembered him as the late editor of the *Woman's World*—a part for which he was singularly unfitted if we are to judge him by the work which he has been allowed to publish in *Lippincott's Magazine,* and which Messrs. Ward, Lock and Co. have not been ashamed to circulate in Great Britain. Not being curious in ordure, and not wishing to offend the nostrils of decent persons, we do not propose to analyse 'The Picture of Dorian Gray'— that would be to advertise the developments of an esoteric prurience. The puzzle is that a young man of decent parts who enjoyed, when he was at Oxford, the opportunity of associating with gentlemen, should put his name—such as it is—to so stupid and vulgar a piece of work. Let nobody read it in the hope of finding witty paradox or racy wickedness. The writer airs his cheap research among the garbage of the French decadents like any drivelling pedant, and he bores you unmercifully with his prosy rigmaroles about the beauty of the body and the corruption of the soul. The grammar is better than Ouida's—the erudition equal; but in every other respect we prefer the talented lady who broke off with pious aposiopesis when she touched upon the horrors which are described in the pages of Suetonius and Livy—not to mention the yet worse infamies believed by many scholars to be accurately portrayed in the lost works of Plutarch, Venus and Nicodemus—especially Nicodemus.

"Let us take one peep at the young men in Mr. Oscar Wilde's story. Puppy No. 1 is the painter of a picture of 'Dorian Gray'; Puppy No. 2 is the critic (a courtesy lord, skilled in all the knowledge of the Egyptians and weary of all the sins and pleasures of London); Puppy No. 3 is the original, cultivated by Puppy No. 1 with a romantic friendship. The Puppies are all talking: Puppy No. 1 about his heart, Puppy No. 2 about his sins and pleasures and the pleasures of sin, and Puppy No. 3 about himself—always about himself and generally about his face, which is brainless and beautiful. The Puppies appear to fill up the intervals of talk by plucking daisies and playing with them, and sometimes by drinking something with strawberries in it. The youngest Puppy is told he is 'charming'; but he mustn't sit in the sun for fear of spoiling his complexion. When he is rebuked for being a naughty, wilful boy he makes a pretty *moue*—this man of twenty! This is how he is addressed by the *blasé* Puppy at their first meeting: 'Yes, Mr. Gray, the gods have been good to you. But what the gods give they quickly take away. When your mouth goes your beauty will go with it, and then you will suddenly discover that there are no triumphs left for you. . . . Time is jealous of you and wars against your lilies and roses. You will become sallow and hollow-cheeked and dull-eyed. You will suffer horribly.'

"Why, bless our souls! haven't we read something of this kind somewhere in the classics? Yes, of course we have! But in what recondite author? Ah, yes!—no!—yes! it was in Horace! What an advantage it is to have received a classical education, and how it will astonish the Yankees. But we must not forget our Puppies, who have probably occupied their time in lapping 'something with strawberries in it.' Puppy No. 1 (the art puppy) has been telling Puppy No. 3 (the dull puppy) how much he admired him. What is the answer? 'I am less to you than your ivory Hermes or your silver Fawn. You will like them always. How long will you like me?—till I have my first wrinkle, I suppose. I know now that when one loses one's good looks, whatever they may be, one loses everything. . . . I am jealous of the portrait you have painted of me. Why should it keep what I must lose? Oh, if it was only the other way! If the picture could only change and I could be always what I am now!'

"No sooner said than done. The picture does change; the original doesn't. Here is a situation for you! Théophile Gautier could have made it romantic—entrancingly beautiful. Mr. Stevenson could have made it convincing, humorous, pathetic. Mr. Anstey could have made it screamingly funny. It has been reserved for Mr. Oscar Wilde to make it dull and nasty. The promising youth plunges into every kind of mean depravity, and ends in being cut by fast women and vicious men; he finishes with murder. . . . And every wickedness or filthiness committed by Dorian Gray is faithfully registered upon his face in the picture; but his living features are undisturbed and unmarred by his inward vileness. This is the story which Mr. Oscar Wilde has tried to tell. A very lame story it is and very lamely it is told.

"Why has he told it? There are two explanations; and, so far as we can see, not more than two.
Not to give pleasure to his readers; the thing is
too clumsy, too tedious and—alas that we should
say it—too stupid! Perhaps it was to shock his
readers in order that they might cry fie upon him
and talk about him. Are we then to suppose that
Mr. Oscar Wilde has yielded to the craving for a
notoriety which he once earned by talking fiddle-
faddle about other men's art, and seize his only
chance of recalling it by making himself obvious at
the cost of being obnoxious and by attracting the
notice which the olfactory sense cannot refuse to
the presence of certain self-asserting organisms?
That is an uncharitable hypothesis, and we would
gladly abandon it. It may be suggested—but is it
more charitable?—that he derives pleasure from
treating a subject merely because it is disgusting.
The phenomenon is not unknown in recent literature, and it takes two forms, in appearance widely
separate—in fact, two branches from the same root
—a root which draws its life from malodorous
putrefaction. One development is found in the
Puritan prurience which produced Tolstoy's 'Kreut-
zer Sonata' and Mr. Stead's famous outbursts.
That is odious enough and mischievous enough, and
it is rightly execrated because it is tainted with a

hypocrisy not the less culpable because charitable people may believe it to be unconscious. But is it more odious or more mischievous than the frank paganism which delights in dirtiness and confesses its delight? Still, they are both chips from the same block—'The Maiden Tribute of Modern Babylon' and 'The Picture of Dorian Gray'—and both of them ought to be chucked into the fire—not so much because they are dangerous and corrupt as because they are incurably silly, written by simple *poseurs* (whether they call themselves puritan or pagan) who know nothing about the life which they affect to have explored and because they are mere catchpenny revelations of the non-existent which, if they reveal anything at all, are revelations only of the singularly unpleasant minds from which they emerge."

The last paragraph is significant as bearing out what I have said with regard to the difference between the public morals of the time when "The Picture of Dorian Gray" was first published and the public morals of to-day. The review as a whole did not please Wilde, and he wrote to the editor of the *St. James' Gazette* to say that he was "quite incapable of understanding how any work of art can be criticised from a moral standpoint." This, plainly, was no answer to the review, nor can it be answered with reasonable argument. A similarly cutting article which appeared in the *Daily Chronicle* described "Dorian Gray" as "a mixture of dullness and dirt"—"a tale spawned from the leprous literature of the French decadents"—"a poisonous book, the atmosphere of which is heavy with the mephitic odours of moral and spiritual putrefaction"—"a gloating study of the mental and physical corruption of a fresh, fair and golden youth." "There is not a single good and holy impulse of human nature, scarcely a fine feeling or instinct that civilisation, art and religion have developed throughout the ages as part of the barriers between Humanity and Animalism that is not held up to ridicule and contempt in 'Dorian Gray,'" continued the *Chronicle*. To which, and a great deal more of similarly scathing comment, Wilde could muster up no better reply than to say: "My story is an essay on decorative art. It reacts against the crude brutality of plain realism. It is poisonous, if you like, but you cannot deny that it is also perfect, and perfection is what we artists aim at."

Neither the *St. James' Gazette* nor the *Daily Chronicle* could foresee that a book which they took to be the outcome of prowlings and garbage-hunting among the French decadents would come to be the gospel and literary stand-by of a world-wide cult of moral and physical leprosy; but the thing has come to pass, and "Dorian Gray" goes on accomplishing its mission, unquestioned by criticism, unchecked by authority, and belauded by every half-baked youth who can earn a precarious shilling by dabbling in ink.

CHAPTER XXIII

W ITH much more wisdom than appears on the surface of the remark, Mr. Ransome tells us in the "Critical Study" that it is "scarcely twenty years since Wilde wrote his books, and in poetry as well as in prose their influence is already becoming so common as not to be recognised." This is true, and true in the worst sense. Every objectionable book that is published at a reasonable price increases the trend—considered impossible at one time in this country, but now obviously marked—towards a want of decency in our national literature. By a singular irony, the criticism of the day is largely in the hands of Radicals and Nonconformists, many of whom, by an irony still more singular, are engaged in the propagation of loose and pernicious doctrine. I would like to wager that the present book will be attacked with the greatest fury in precisely the quarters where, twenty years ago, it would have been applauded. If I wish to see Wilde and his work spoken of with the greatest respect and the greatest admiration, I have nothing to do but turn to certain Radical or Nonconformist sheets, and I shall be at once obliged. I am of opinion that certain novels, and even certain magazines and reviews, now published in England would never have existed at all but for Oscar Wilde. One of the monthly reviews is a particular offender; and the infection is not limited to one paper only. Nobody seems to be shocked or distressed by the fact and nobody lifts a voice or a pen by way of complaint. The journals I have in my mind are, in the main, respectable and reasonably cultivated publications. They are above purchase or corruption in regard to their general conduct, being owned by rich men or syndicates and run in some instances at a loss or, at any rate, no particular profit, and for the good of the political interests they represent. They take a high tone with regard to political and social morality. They contain general articles, stories, sketches and so forth which are beyond reproach both as regards their tone and literary qualities. Yet when it comes to dealing with literature itself they may be found only too frequently on the side of the palpably dubious and undesirable.

I have had several years of editorial experience of my own, and out of that experience I think I can

explain the phenomenon. It simply amounts to
this: Editors are too busy—or too careless—to
select their reviewers judiciously and, when a book
has been reviewed, they are too busy or too careless
to examine the reviewer's work with a view to
making sure that it is free from the current taints.
It is a fact that the younger school of critics, and
many of the old ones, now base themselves on
Wilde's dictum that a work of art cannot be criticised from a moral standpoint, and that the sphere
of art and the sphere of ethics are absolutely distinct and separate. If the result were that the
reviewer contented himself with the consideration
of literary work *quâ* art, and in no other relation,
there would perhaps be no great harm done; but
in point of fact this is seldom or never done, and
it is next door to impossible that it should be done.
Opinions and moral reflections insist on finding
their way even into works of art, and literary works
of art are, by their very nature, almost entirely
made up of them. In spite of his own denial of the
inter-relation between art and morals, Wilde always
asserted that "Dorian Gray" had a moral—that is
to say, when it suited him to make the assertion.
It is obvious that any four lines of serious verse
must have some sort of a moral bearing, and so
every poem has a moral and every story has a moral

and every piece of writing has a moral—implied, even if it be not specifically stated. Now the new reviewer and all of the old ones know this as well as I do. They cannot divide art from morality, and when they pretend to do so it will usually be found that they are really condoning, defending, upholding or propagating obvious immorality. I do not wish it to be supposed that the review columns of English journals bristle with this sort of thing; but there can be no doubt that it crops up from time to time and with a sufficient frequency to make it quite plain that the press is far more easy and tolerant on the matter than it has any right to be. Obviously, letters is a vehicle which is handier than any other vehicle for the spread of evil thinking. An improper picture is improper on the face of it, and calls immediate attention to itself and immediate reproof from decent people. Such pictures cannot really exist publicly. An improper play has to get past the censor, and it has also to overcome the repugnance of persons who do not like openly to be assisting in wickedness. Both picture and play, too, have to be, in the nature of things, either decent, or frankly and palpably indecent. But in a book you can have dubiety, and you can have patches of impropriety and indecency tucked away amid a mass of inoffensive and, it may be, even excellent writing. This is particularly the case with regard to novels and poetry, and nobody with any care for either literature or the public well-being can help but regret it. The only censorship which can do anything to stem the increasing tide of looseness and license in these regards is, obviously, criticism. I maintain that the criticism of the day is—in a preponderating measure, consciously or unconsciously—in agreement with Wilde on these subjects, and the result is plain for all of us to see. I used to believe that art is more important than conduct. This is a mistake which most of us are prone to make when we are young and dazzled with the beauty and colour of life. The vast mass of mankind, however, are not concerned with art as art at all, but merely with art in its relation to its personal effect upon themselves. The average reader, whether of prose or verse, has little or no conscious interest in the art of either. If he had, many of the moderns with enormous circulations would feel a very considerable draught, inasmuch as they are not artists and do not pretend to be. In view of the general ability to read and the extraordinary cheapness of books, it has become more than ever important that literature should be kept free from viciousness, prurience and improper suggestion. If criticism fails in its duty in this respect, the national intellect and the national morals will inevitably be debased, and the proper purposes of art utterly destroyed. It is the fashion to say that great authors do not write merely for youth and young misses at school, but it is neverthe-less a fact that it is upon the adolescent of both sexes that these authors have to depend, in the main, for a hearing and for reputation and income. In the case of Wilde, it is to youth particularly that he very largely appeals. Most persons of middle life know a great deal more about the facts of existence than would admit them to take Wilde for anything but a flippant and unbalanced writer. The wise perceive that there is no gingerbread beneath his gilt, and they know that even the gilt is not honest metal. His influence upon youth is un-doubted and obvious, but it is equally undoubted and obvious that his influence is a bad one, and the sooner we acknowledge the fact the better it will be for Art and Letters.

CHAPTER XXIV

TO be properly understood in this world is beyond human expectation. That my relations with Wilde have been misunderstood this narrative bears witness. Pretty well everything I have done or said with respect to him has been misconstrued or misrepresented; and, of course, it was not a matter of surprise to me to find that when Crosland published "The First Stone" some devotees took it for granted that I had suborned him to do it. Their rage knew no bounds. On the appearance of the book, half the editors in London were besieged with letters from adherents of Wilde—whose identity was and is entirely unknown to me—abusing Crosland and explaining that it was well known that I had instigated him to write the work, and paid for the publication. So far as I am aware, none of these letters was printed and, when the writers of them found that they could not get the publicity they required, they took to sending copies of them to Crosland and myself.

Ultimately somebody went to the length of printing a pamphlet in which both of us were accused of all sorts of vileness. This pamphlet appeared without the name of its author and without the name or address of the printer and publisher. Those responsible for it lacked the courage of their opinions, but they had pluck enough to post it out under cover and to say that copies of it could be obtained at some address in Chelsea. I had enquiries made at the address given and found that it consisted of a block of flats, but that there was nobody there who would admit any knowledge of the matter. The pamphlet was called "The Writing on the Floor," but nobody who lived on any of the floors of these flats from the basement upwards, would own to the slightest connection with it. I mention these facts not because I attach any importance to the pamphlet, but because they show to what extraordinary courses my enemies will have resort when their malice gets the better of them. They indicate, too, that there is no limit to the resources of these people. The difficulties of obtaining a printer, whether in London or the provinces, for such statements as were contained in "The Writing on the Floor" must have been well-nigh insuperable. No printer who can read could, in ordinary circumstances, have been procured to produce such a pamphlet, even without his *imprimatur*, on any terms whatever. He would know full well that the risks were too great. More crass and abominable criminal libels were never put into type. The thing could only have been printed either abroad or at a private press; and, from the character of the type and paper, I should say that the chances are that the printing was done at a private press in England. The type was new and the paper such as is readily obtainable in London. All this meant considerable cost, upon which the authors of the pamphlet could not hope to recoup themselves, inasmuch as they gave it away and did not set a price upon it; besides which there was a cost of postage and clerical work. So that we had here not only malice and wicked propaganda, but malice and wicked propaganda which were willing to go to great expense and to run great risks for the expression of themselves. This business, and other similar businesses which have come to my notice, tend to convince me that there are plenty of minor enthusiasts engaged in the canonisation of Wilde, and that they lack neither means nor energy. I use the phrase "minor enthusiast" advisedly because I wish to make it clear that I do not suggest that any person named in this book was a party to these letters or anonymous scurrilities.

With regard to "The First Stone" itself, I have
no wish to apologise for it, and should not have the
slightest objection to accepting the responsibility
for it—if it were mine to accept. But it is not mine,
nor did I suggest or advise it, or have hand or part
in its production. What happened was this: When
I obtained through my solicitors a copy of the unpublished parts of "De Profundis," duly authenticated by Messrs. Lewis & Lewis, I took it, without
reading it, to Mr. Crosland. I did this of my own
initiative and for my own reasons. Crosland began
to read it in my presence. He had not read more
than a page or two before he said: "I am going to
read this manuscript to you, word for word, and
I am going to put absolutely flat and straight questions to you, even though they hurt or anger you."
I said: "You can read away, my dear chap, and ask
me any questions you like." I sat there for four
solid hours, face to face with the man who probably
knows more about me and my life and my manner
of living it than anybody else in the world, and I
am free to say that he did not spare me. But it is
necessary to remember that, up to this time, Crosland had never had any other version of the history
and my connection with Wilde than my own. When
he first met me in 1903, over the publication of some
of my sonnets, we had not talked together three

minutes before he plumped me with some sharp
questions in regard to myself and Wilde. I was
able at once to give him straightforward and convincing answers and, in good times and bad, from
that day to this, he has believed me, as, indeed, he
could not help but believe me, and he has always
and rightly acted on the assumption that he knew
the truth. But I remembered those questions of
his, and it was partly for this reason, namely, that
I courted all the questions he could devise, that I
went round to him with the unpublished "De Profundis." Here was new material of which neither
he nor I had ever had the smallest inkling. I knew
that it could not be friendly material, otherwise it
would not have been put up by Ransome's solicitors,
yet I placed it unreservedly in the hands of my closest
friend, a critically minded person of whom it may be
said, at least, that neither friendship nor any other
consideration will hold or restrain him where matters of principle are concerned. After reading the
manuscript Crosland went to work of his own accord and, within a very few days, "The First Stone"
was written and printed. Whatever may be its
merits or faults as a piece of writing, it is certainly
of interest as exhibiting the effect on an honest mind
of Wilde's stupid and ludicrous outburst. I am not
concerned either to praise or blame the poem, but

it will last Wilde probably a good deal longer than the unpublished parts of "De Profundis" will last me. I had intended to republish the whole poem in this book, but as it contains quotations taken direct from the unpublished portion of "De Profundis," I have been reluctantly compelled to abandon my intention.

CHAPTER XXV

I DO not know what Mr. Robert Ross's legal rights as Wilde's literary executor were until the year 1906, when his position was officially confirmed. During the last years of his life Wilde certainly looked to me to do all that might be necessary to be done in regard to his literary affairs after his death. Ross knew this, and other people knew it. Both Wilde and I, however, had been accustomed to look upon him as a business man, and I quite admit that when he came to me after the funeral and asked me what should be done with Wilde's papers, I told him to act as he thought fit. The first occasion upon which Ross used the title of literary executor was in Paris after the funeral. Somebody in an English paper had suggested that Wilde had been buried without ceremony and that none of his friends had thought it worth while to attend the funeral. I considered that this was an improper statement, and a long telegram was written and sent to the paper in question, the *Daily*

Express, with a view to its correction. The question arose as to whether I should sign it or whether somebody else should sign it, and in the end we decided that the signature should be Ross's. After Ross had put his name to the telegram he said to me: "It will carry more weight if I were to put 'Literary executor to Oscar Wilde' under my name." I saw no objection to this at the time, and Ross added the words, and the telegram was despatched so signed. So far as I am aware, that is the only mandate Ross ever had from anybody. I do not doubt that his position has been confirmed and made legal since by the Receiver of Wilde's estate and by Wilde's sons. Neither do I doubt that Ross has rendered valuable services to the estate and administered it justly and well. I think that he has done many things which are scarcely in Wilde's interest, however, and of which Wilde would have disapproved; such, for example, as his publication of the version of the "Ballad of Reading Gaol," curtailed "for the benefit of reciters and their audiences," and his dedication of "Intentions" to a woman whom Wilde scarcely knew, in his own name rather than Wilde's. But these are minor matters, and there is no need to labour them. The challenge I have to issue to Mr. Ross has to do with the question of "De Profundis."

It is admitted by all parties concerned that this manuscript was addressed to me. A portion of the work has already been published, under Mr. Ross's sanction. The other half he has presented to the nation through the British Museum. So that it is evident that Mr. Ross feels that the whole manuscript should be preserved. Sufficient of the contents of the second or unpublished part has been made public in the Law Courts and in the press to make it quite obvious that the manuscript relates chiefly to me, and relates to me in a very bitter, malicious and libellous way. It is consequently a document in which at least two living persons are very seriously concerned. Neither Mr. Ross nor any other person dare print or publish the thing as it stands, because of its libellous character, and they know quite well that, apart from any action I might take, the Dowager Marchioness of Queensberry would be absolutely sure to take action against them if the manuscript were published. Mr. Ross therefore stores this libel at the British Museum till 1960, when, in the course of human events, my mother will have passed away and I, too, shall be dead. At this happy juncture the discretion of the British Museum authorities is to come into play. As a matter of fact, however, the manuscript will be out of copyright by 1960 and, unless the British

Museum destroy it meanwhile—which, by the way, they would not be within their legal rights in doing —there is nothing to hinder publication, inasmuch as it is open knowledge that copies exist and are in other hands than those of the British Museum. Now I think it will be commonly admitted that a person who is attacked possesses *de facto* the right to reply; furthermore, it is the duty of a person who knows that he has been accused, as I have been accused, to defend and clear himself, if he can. Therefore it is that I conceive it to be my duty thoroughly to sift and examine the charges which Oscar Wilde has brought against me, and to rebut them and give proof that they are false and unsubstantial. It is impossible that this can be done completely and satisfactorily unless I have from Mr. Ross, who, rightly or wrongly, considers himself the legal owner of the copyright, permission to print very lengthy portions of the manuscript now in the hands of the British Museum. In view of the subtle way in which the manuscript is written, it would not be sufficient for my purpose to make extracts here and there and deal with them singly. The only proper method, in the circumstances, would be to print the unpublished "De Profundis" *in extenso,* with my running comment, either beneath it or on the opposite pages. Mr. Ross is acquainted with the whole

contents of this manuscript, and he contends that
he is the owner of the copyright. I challenge him
to give his permission for the manuscript to be used
in the manner I have indicated. My proposition is
a perfectly fair and square one. I will publish the
whole manuscript, word for word and line for line,
without omitting or curtailing anything, and over it
I will publish my reply, and the public at large shall
be left to judge between Oscar Wilde and Lord
Alfred Douglas. Mr. Ross's acquiescence in this
proposal cannot hurt him in the least. Nobody has
anything to gain out of the manuscript, inasmuch as
Mr. Ross dare not publish it himself, or get anybody else to publish it, in my lifetime or the lifetime of my mother. He knows that it is a libel on
both of us, and the least he can do if he is a fair-
minded man is to give me an opportunity of dealing
openly and fully with the accusations involved. If
he refuses to do this, I take it that the public will
draw their own conclusions as to the truth or falsity
of these accusations.

CHAPTER XXVI

A STOCK argument of Wilde's critical friends has always been that, even if it can be demonstrated that Wilde has been grossly overrated in England, the fact of his popularity in foreign parts proves that there is in him the literary stuff which goes to the making of immortals. This, of course, is not philosophically true, being, in fact, the merest fudge. Wilde's books, it is true, have been translated into various languages—but which books? Well, "Dorian Gray" and "Salome," for the most part, with "De Profundis" for a bad third, and the rest nowhere. What Wilde abroad really means is very prettily indicated by the following letter which was addressed to the editor of *Everyman* by one of Wilde's translators:—

"Sir,

"Please let me produce some figures to uphold your correspondent's statement in your issue of June 6th as to Oscar Wilde's popularity in Russia.

"I have had the honour of translating Wilde's

works into Russian and can state that his books were among the best-selling fiction in this country. Some of Oscar Wilde's masterpieces, such as 'The Picture of Dorian Gray,' 'De Profundis,' 'Salome,' published in popular editions at 10 kopecks (2½d.) each have had a circulation (in the last four to five years) from eighty to one hundred thousand each, and are still selling briskly. Wilde's comedies are constantly on the repertory of the Moscow and St. Petersburg Imperial State Theatres, not counting the innumerable provincial stages.

"I can assure you that you will not find one educated person in Russia who has not read Wilde's works. I have received in the last seven to eight years hundreds of letters from quite unknown people all over Russia, with the expression of the strongest and sincerest admiration for one of 'the greatest writers of the world.'

"I must frankly acknowledge that nearly all the letters of my correspondents, ranking from all classes of Russian life, contain many bitter comments on the treatment Wilde received in the hands of his countrymen.

"I am, Sir, etc.,

"MICHAEL LYKIARDOPULOS,

"Secretary of the

"Moscow."   " 'Moscow Art Theatre.'

This letter gives a curious insight into the whole business. Of course, "Dorian Gray" and "Salome" at twopence-halfpenny in England would sell like wildfire, just as a pirated "De Profundis" was sold a little while ago at a penny on the street corners. Nobody professed that this pirated "De Profundis" was being sold because of its literary value: it was sold and offered for sale in the gutter as "the confession of Oscar Wilde," and it was bought in just the same way that the alleged confession of any other criminal would be bought. So that these books at ten kopecks in Russia point their own moral.

I do not know how cheaply or how dearly Wilde is sold in Paris and Berlin. But I do know that the vogue he has in both cities is largely based on his iniquities, and that this fact is equally deplored by right-thinking Frenchmen and right-thinking Germans. In the scandals which of late years have disgraced Berlin, the Wilde factor has been only too evident. The scandals to which I refer have occurred in so-called literary and artistic circles; and wherever you have such scandals in such circles there you are bound always to find that Oscar Wilde sits enthroned. It is a deplorable thing, doubtless, but what is one to expect in the face of "Dorian Gray"? The bad influence of Wilde in both France and Germany has been noted and deprecated by more than one eminent writer, and the main force of criticism in both countries is in arms against it. In Russia his admirers belong chiefly to the anarchistic and revolutionary sections of the community, who, being in a large measure decadents and criminals themselves, have a natural sympathy with the work of a decadent criminal. In Russia they say Wilde must be a great man because he went to prison and is universally loved and admired by the English. In England we are told that Wilde's greatness cannot be disputed, inasmuch as he is loved and admired in Russia—at 10 kopecks a time.

Mr. Ransome is very amusing on Wilde's foreign successes. He says that we "cannot afford to neglect the opinion of critical Germany," which, in point of fact, is just the opinion we can afford to neglect; and he quotes Mr. Ross as follows: "In 1901, within a year of the author's death, it ("Salome") was produced in Berlin; from that moment it has held the European stage. It has run for a longer consecutive period in Germany than any play by any Englishman, not excepting Shakespeare. Its popularity has extended to all countries where it is not prohibited. It is performed throughout Europe, Asia and America. It is played even in Yiddish." One would imagine

that all Europe, Asia and America had rushed in
a body to see this compelling drama. The facts
are that, while it may have been staged at theatres
of standing in Berlin and other cities, and may
have had a long run in Berlin, its vogue elsewhere
is not associated with either distinguished theatres
or the best actors, having been, in fact, a rather
hole-and-corner affair, and, whatever may have happened years ago, one may travel the globe nowadays without finding that Wilde comes anywhere
near holding the stage in a substantial or perennial
way. Wilde, of course, has been pushed and
boomed for all he is worth and for a good deal more
than he is worth. The result is that he has come
into a sort of artificial kingdom of his own, on the
Continent and in America just as in England. But
I maintain that it is a kingdom based on rottenness;
that it is an utterly insignificant kingdom in so far
as it is taken to mean merit or worthiness in Wilde,
and that, by its very nature, it is bound to fall and
be forgotten. Wilde's supporters would appear to
be very conscious of this fact, and that is perhaps
why some of them fall into such fits of rage if anybody ventures to suggest that their idol is not entirely gold. There are no plays of Wilde's and no
books of Wilde's which can last on their literary
merits. His only chance is that he suffered im-

prisonment and he wrote certain improprieties. These have been put on a different basis for an enduring literary reputation, even in Asia or among the Jews.

CHAPTER XXVII

THE SMALLER FRY

I SUPPOSE that the number of little poets, little fictionists, and, above all, little critics, who imagine that they owe themselves to Wilde is infinite. His peculiar form of humour, which seemed to have genius behind it and so dazzled everybody in Wilde's own time, was soon discovered to be wonderfully easy of imitation, and really to require very little brains in its production. The consequence has been that everybody who considered himself anybody took up with it, as it were; and it has become so common that it is no longer taken for humour at all. All our dullest young men who happen to be engaged or interested in a branch of the arts have talked, thought and written Wilde for years past. Some middle-aged and elderly gentlemen who began when Wilde was at his zenith are still at it, and apparently nothing will stop them; which means, of course, that humour in England has altogether lost both its point and its usefulness. The humour of the day has a dull cruelty about

it which it formerly lacked. Its object might almost
be, not to make people laugh, but to make them cry.
The fiercer and more heartless it is, the better it is
supposed to be appreciated. Furthermore, instead
of being kept in its proper place in the scheme of
things, it has been allowed to run riot whenever
its authors choose to let it loose. To be comic in
a bitter and insincere way seems to be the ambition
of most of the eminent people one can nowadays
come across. We have comic judges and comic
counsel who manage to keep the King's Courts in
ripples of merriment. We have even a comic magistrate or two. In Parliament the mordant humourist and the man who can say sharp things are the
only ones to be listened to; sarcastic bishops and
witty clerics abound. And as for the gentlemen of
the press, they are all bent on the leer, at whatever
cost. If you look closely into these professed or un-
professed fun-makers, you are bound to perceive
that the majority of them are little Oscar Wildes
to a man. They look on life with a confirmed squint
and they cannot see that there is anything human
about which it is not desirable that they should
make jokes. Only a little while back we had the
spectacle of an English judge indulging his fancy
in Wildeisms in the course of a trial for murder.
In itself, his Lordship's epigram or paradox, or

whatever you like to call it, would help or hurt no-body; but the fact that it was forthcoming in such circumstances indicates pretty plainly the pass to which we have come.

Wilde's answer to everything was by quip or fleer, or a plain perversion of the truth. He had no serious views or intentions about anything, and he considered that the art of life lay in flippancy. People who read him and make a gospel of him can scarcely be expected not to imitate him, and imitate him they certainly do; so that nowadays we have hundreds of little Wildes where formerly there was only one Wilde—and a not over big one at that. They swarm and spread themselves over everything that is decent, and they parrot Wilde at everybody who comes near them. They have seen it in "Intentions" that there is no sin save stupidity, and that all art is immoral, and they imagine that the world can be run on these two remarkably shallow and unreliable axioms.

I am quite free to admit that in a literary sense the world does present the appearance of being so run. The preponderating weight of contemporary authorship and criticism would indeed seem to be on the Wilde side. This, of course, is unthinkably pitiable, but we cannot get beyond the fact. The reason is not far to seek, and it will be found to lie in the shallowness which always characterises the popular view of large questions. Wilde began by asserting that the only sin was stupidity, yet he ended with the assertion that the supreme vice is shallowness. I do not say that shallowness is by any means the supreme vice; there can be no doubt, however, that it is the very commonest vice among people who imagine themselves to be thinkers. It is, in consequence of this very circumstance, that to attack Wilde nowadays is to be howled down, just as to have praised him eighteen years ago was to be execrated. The shallowness of 1895 could not see an inch below the surface of Wilde's glaring viciousness. It went the length of taking his name off his own plays and relegating him to the position of a man who was well-nigh without literary existence. The shallowness of 1914 is unable to look beneath the success, enormous sales, enormous popularity, and what not, which have resulted from the Wilde boom, and it is quite incapable of recognising or appreciating the dangers which lie beneath it. We are asked by tearful counsel and writers of pathetic nonsense for the penny weeklies to forget Wilde's vices. For my own part, I certainly do not wish to revive them or insist upon them. But I am not prepared to forget them unless his apologists cease to discuss them.

Nobody will question that what has been termed the revulsion of feeling in Wilde's favour was largely brought about by the publication of "De Profundis." This book, which, as I have shown, does not in the least accurately represent Wilde's feelings, owes its success in no small measure to the wide publicity which was given to the statements that it had been written in prison, and that it is a sort of repentant confession and authentic dying speech of its author. As we have seen, and as will become still more apparent when the unpublished "De Profundis" sees the light, nothing can be further from the truth. The small fry may go on admiring Wilde, and they may go on pointing to "De Profundis" as a work of a sainted martyr—the swan-song of a contrite, broken and bleeding heart, and so on, as long as they please. But they will never get away from the hard facts of the case, which are quite the reverse of what has been generally assumed and supposed.

CHAPTER XXVIII

TO BE DONE WITH IT ALL

WHEN Wilde had completed the "De Profundis" manuscript, he is understood to have written to Ross to say that he had rid his bosom of much perilous stuff. I will do him the justice to agree that he got into the "De Profundis" manuscript as a whole, more real Wilde than ever he put into any other piece of work. Before, he had given us, as far as in him lay, Wilde the artist with frequent glimpses of Wilde the shameful liver and vicious thinker. But in the complete "De Profundis" he gives us Wilde the man. The bottom of his vicious and halting soul is laid bare for us in this extraordinary work. That he had it in him to give himself utterly and entirely away as he did is incomprehensible, and can only be set down to the fact that the reticence which had previously been his safeguard and saviour was entirely destroyed by his rage on perceiving that the life he had succeeded in living would never again be possible to him.

My own task is finished here and now. I have taken what is practically Wilde's own picture of himself and unveiled it. Before he went to prison he had exposed to the public gaze a picture of himself which was all lights and rose and purple. To this picture his friends have been most faithful. Of their own initiative they decked it out with supererogatory daubs of pretty and bewitching colour; and they set it round with a beautiful gold frame, surmounted with a crown of gilded bays and something which is intended for a halo. Of the shadows and dubious blacks and browns which Wilde himself prepared by his life and by his lucubrations in gaol they have been anxious to take no notice. They were only brought out of their seclusion as weapons wherewith I might be defeated. The pot of blackness was brought into a Court of Justice and there emptied before the gaze of all beholders, as was supposed, for my upsetting. Then the mess was all scraped up, as best it could be, and hurried back to the British Museum; and, honour being now satisfied and all being over, everybody, it was hoped, would speedily forget the little black pot. But not so: it will never be forgotten and must always be remembered by anybody who wishes to look honestly at the features of Wilde.

So far as I am concerned, I have drawn my own

picture from the man as I knew him, and from his writings, which are readily accessible and can be pursued by all who care to take the trouble. If I had been disposed to write the present book in the vein of "De Profundis," published or unpublished, it would not have been difficult, from a literary point of view, for me to do so. I could have embellished my pages with tears and regrets and moral reflections, not to say with quotations from the classics and Holy Scripture, just as readily and at just as great length as Wilde has done. Surely if any man has had cause for tears and bitter regrets, I have had cause. All my life, from twenty years of age up, has been overshadowed and filled with scandal and grief through my association with this man, Oscar Wilde. I am not going to shed public or private tears about it, and I am not going to waste my breath in vain regrets. I have absolutely an easy conscience as regards my treatment of Wilde, both before and since his death. If I have hurt anybody at all it has been myself and my family, and I have done this only through misplaced loyalty to my friend and a too high regard for chivalry. I now say all that I have had to say about Wilde, whether with respect to my personal relationship to him or my mature view of his complete writings. It will be noted that, just as I have refrained from weeping and moralising, I have equally refrained from details of petty quarrels and misunderstandings. I have not accused him of gobbling my food and spilling my wine and devouring my substance; I have not charged him, as I easily might, with corrupting my intellect and assisting me in the careless waste of some of the best years of my life. I have never said, as he says of me, that I became a child in his hands and that we never met "except in the gutter," and never conversed except about "loathsome things." I hold that a man's acts are his own affairs, even if they lead to his ruin and disgrace. The shifting of responsibility is no work for me or any other person of sense. I accept full responsibility for everything I have done or said in regard to this affair. For my own indiscretions and carelessness I could not honestly blame anybody. I have been punished for them and shall doubtless go on being punished for them; but there they are, and all the water in the sea will not wash them out. This book is not an apology for me, neither is it a work undertaken on the *tu quoque* or tit-for-tat principle against Wilde. I am of opinion that, in the circumstances, there is no man living who can put Oscar Wilde into his true relation to the life and literature of his time more accurately than myself. I have always known this—though, at the same time, I have hitherto refrained from putting my pen to paper. My enemies have compelled me to defend myself, and if, in the course of that defence, I have had to tear away some of the undeserved laurels which have been heaped upon his brow and dissipated some of the undeserved incense which has been offered up at his shrine, I have done him no wrong, and I feel that I may conceivably have made a slight contribution to the literary and general good.

It seems to me a great deal more than probable that the present volume will rouse a considerable deal of what is called controversy. The right of criticism is everybody's right, and I shall not hope to be spared criticism or, for that matter, even contradiction. I shall only beg that those reviewers whose duty and business it will be to deal with this book may remember that I am entitled to exactly as much justice in this world as Wilde and Wilde's friends. The forces against me are undoubtedly numerous and powerful. On the other hand, it is very certain that I shall not run away from them.

Index

Reprint Publishing

For People Who Go For Originals.

This book is a facsimile reprint of the original edition. The term refers to the facsimile with an original in size and design exactly matching simulation as photographic or scanned reproduction.

Facsimile editions offer us the chance to join in the library of historical, cultural and scientific history of mankind, and to redis-cover.

The books of the facsimile edition may have marks, notations and other margi-nalia and pages with errors contained in the original volume. These traces of the past refers to the historical journey that has covered the book.

ISBN 978-3-95940-273-6

Made in Germany

www.reprintpublishing.com